GREAT AMERICAN PROPHETS

POPE FRANCIS'S MODELS OF CHRISTIAN LIFE

Daniel Cosacchi

Paulist Press
New York / Mahwah, NJ

Cover and book design by Lynn Else

Library of Congress Cataloging-in-Publication Data
Names: Cosacchi, Daniel, author.
Title: Great American prophets : Pope Francis's models of Christian life / Daniel Cosacchi.
Description: New York / Mahwah : Paulist Press, [2022] | Includes index. | Summary: "Using the examples of the "Great Americans" cited by Pope Francis during his visit to the United States, Daniel Cosacchi discusses how prophecy can be manifested in our own time" — Provided by publisher.
Identifiers: LCCN 2022012682 (print) | LCCN 2022012683 (ebook) | ISBN 9780809155729 (paperback) | ISBN 9781587689710 (ebook)
Subjects: LCSH: Francis, Pope, 1936– | Prophecy. | Prophets. | Americans. | United States.
Classification: LCC BX1378.7 .C68 2022 (print) | LCC BX1378.7 (ebook) | DDC 282.092 — dc23/eng/20220801
LC record available at https://lccn.loc.gov/2022012682
LC ebook record available at https://lccn.loc.gov/2022012683

ISBN 978-0-8091-5572-9 (paperback)
ISBN 978-1-58768-971-0 (e-book)

Published by Paulist Press
997 Macarthur Boulevard
Mahwah, New Jersey 07430
www.paulistpress.com

Printed and bound in the
United States of America

To Julia

CONTENTS

FOREWORD

Blessings are not always easy to recognize or honor; it is why prophets can be so helpful.

While unquestionably a blessing as far as vocations go, it can be arduous to be a woman formed by Catholic social teaching, living in the United States of America, working to strengthen the Catholic Church and call it to greater levels of trustworthiness, accountability, and effective stewardship. These have not been easy days or years to be a Catholic in America who wants to believe, as Pope Francis does, that politics is the highest form of love, or *caritas*. I admit to times of feeling politically and religiously homeless, caring as deeply as I do in the worthiness of active civic engagement in pursuit of a more perfect union, and baptismal responsibility to advocate for the role of the laity, especially women, in the Church.

Political acrimony, divisiveness in our country (and in our Church), and leaders displaying ignoble, demeaning, vainglorious behavior have conspired to leave American Catholics who yearn for justice and peace, whose faith and civic duty compels them to advance the common good, feeling bereft. This temptation to dispiritedness has only grown more acute in recent years, particularly in light of serious challenges to the health and well-being of the common good. We are emerging from the COVID-19 pandemic amid other pandemics—of racial injustice, of growing inequity and disparity, of environmental degradation, and of gun violence in the United States.

But now something that feels like a miracle has happened. Daniel Cosacchi has written this book vividly evoking a spectacularly meaningful day for Americans, especially American Catholics, when we were reminded of a rich history and called to a compassionate future. On that day, September 24, 2015, Pope Francis delivered a seminal speech and made history as the first pope to address a joint session of Congress in Washington, D.C.

Great American Prophets is a great gift. I was at the Capitol that momentous day, with two dear friends, one of whom has also published a book about Pope Francis. We had seats on the lower west terrace of the Capitol under a glorious blue sky. What I remember most are the four individuals from our U.S. history the pope lifted up in his speech—Abraham Lincoln, Martin Luther King Jr., Dorothy Day, and Thomas Merton—and the invitation to emulate them. But I also remember how truly and unusually proud I was on that day to be Catholic and to be American.

This book brings back vivid, helpful memories of that day and what Pope Francis has called us, as Americans and people of good will, to be and do. It is a further gift that the author elucidates the prophetic stance not only of the four role models identified by the pope in his historic address, but of others to whom we can look for inspiration. What a joy to be given this treatise on prophecy, to be offered so many examples of women as prophets and role models, including friends and longtime personal heroines, and to be given insight into Pope Francis himself, as a vitally important, prophetic leader on the global stage. How fortunate we were to welcome Pope Francis to the United States. How fortunate we are to have this book—a balm for the soul—to help guide us, with inspiration and instruction, to act upon the urgent, moral invitation to be truly great Americans.

Kerry Alys Robinson
Founding Executive Director and Partner
Leadership Roundtable

PREFACE

This book has many potential beginnings. In perhaps the most obvious way, it begins on the floor of the House Chamber of the United States Capitol on September 24, 2015. On that auspicious day, Pope Francis made history by becoming the first pope to address a joint session of Congress. In so doing, he delivered one of the most historically important addresses of his pontificate and presented the motivation for the pages that follow in this volume. The book could also trace its roots to September 22, 1862, when Abraham Lincoln delivered an even more famous statement, perhaps the most famous executive order in American history: the Emancipation Proclamation. In issuing these words, Lincoln ensured that his presidential tenure would be remembered even by a figure such as Pope Francis, over a century later. A century after Lincoln, on August 28, 1963, another speech destined to have greater impact than Francis's—and to which this book could also trace its origins—was Martin Luther King Jr's crowning moment. Speaking from the steps of the Lincoln Memorial to 250,000 people attending the March on Washington for Jobs and Freedom, King spoke the words for which he is most remembered: "I have a dream." Or the book could trace its genesis to either of two conversions that took place in the twentieth century: Catholicism in America has no two more interesting or charismatic converts in that century than Dorothy Day and Thomas Merton. But the book does not begin at any of those historic moments, or even in the United States.

This book begins on the central loggia of St. Peter's Basilica, overlooking the great square where thousands of Romans and international pilgrims gathered to welcome the new pontiff on March 13, 2013. It also begins in an apartment in the Edgewater neighborhood of Chicago. From those quarters, I was holding vigil around the clock in anticipation of the election of Pope Benedict XVI's successor as the Bishop of Rome. In the moments leading up to the election, I was joined by one of my colleagues, Karen Ross, from the theology department at Loyola University Chicago, where we were then graduate students. We had been following the events of this papal transition very closely (okay, obsessively) ever since Benedict had shocked the world by announcing his resignation on February 11, 2013.[1] Like many others who had been reading and watching the news of those unprecedented days in Catholic history, we had a list of *papabile* intermixed with a few of our personal favorite candidates. Even though we were operating a friendly departmental pool with a small payday for one lucky bettor, no one seriously considered Cardinal Jorge Mario Bergoglio a likely candidate. He didn't know enough languages, we thought, plus he was on the verge of retirement, and as he hadn't won in 2005, his chances at St. Peter's chair seemed already far spent.[2]

When Cardinal Jean Louis Taran announced Bergoglio's name, however, our attention immediately shifted to his chosen new name: Francis. That was different; it caught us by the heart and held our gaze as the new pope stepped into view. In his 2005 report of the conclave that had elected Joseph Ratzinger as Pope Benedict XVI, the veteran *Vaticanista* John Allen recounts Bergoglio's runner-up finish in that voting, with these words that appear shocking to us today: "Despite that support, some cardinals candidly doubted that Bergoglio really had the steel and 'fire in the belly' needed to lead the universal church."[3] Even though many traditionalist Catholics have objected to any number of Francis's pontifical statements or actions, today few would remark that he lacked the resolve to carry them out. The name Francis, then, not only pays homage to the great medieval saint of Assisi, but it also offers a programmatic statement about Pope Francis's priorities for the Church. As with any pope who selects a papal name, such a decision is an indication of what is most important to him.

In the case of Pope Francis, choosing the name was an early indicator of the direction that his pontificate would take. In the days after he was elected as the successor to St. Peter, there was much public interest regarding the motivation for his chosen name. As a member of the Society of Jesus, many commentators believed it was in honor of

St. Francis Xavier, one of the original members of the new pope's own religious congregation. However, Pope Francis soon confirmed the name had come from the saintly man of Assisi. Why did the pontiff choose this figure for his patron? In the early days of his papacy, he explained the rationale for such a decision: "For me, [Francis of Assisi] is the man of poverty, the man of peace, the man who loves and protects creation; these days we do not have a very good relationship with creation, do we? He is the man who gives us this spirit of peace, the poor man.... How I would like a Church which is poor and for the poor!"[4]

Francis's priorities have become the priorities of the Church universal in the years since his election. He has continued to emphasize these priorities in various writings, addresses, and homilies.[5] These statements are essential for understanding how Francis wishes to communicate to the Church and the world. Even more essential, though, are the Church's actions in these key areas. On this front, Francis's effectiveness is up for debate, especially in the United States. As most close observers of the U.S. Church have noticed, the standard operating procedure among the American hierarchy has not changed very much in the years since Francis has been elected. While Francis clearly has established a "hands-on" manner of proceeding regarding appointments to major metropolitan sees,[6] the majority of U.S. bishops he has appointed have fallen into similar ideological models as those of his two immediate predecessors. In fact, many of the bishops appointed by Pope Francis self-identify as more theologically conservative than those appointed by his predecessors. As a study conducted by the Center of Applied Research for the Apostolate (CARA) reported, "Pope Francis' emphasis in selecting bishops is based on their having a pastoral orientation, which is not dependent on a particular theological orientation."[7]

While having pastoral bishops is a good and necessary goal in the Church, it can also mean potential for pushback to Francis's agenda, since these bishops can often be more conservative in ideology. So, while Francis is advocating for an ecclesial movement to curb injustices against the poor, peace, and creation, relatively few American bishops are prioritizing these issues in their local churches. If they do not emphasize Francis's concerns, then the timeless philosophical question must be asked yet again: If a tree falls in the forest and no one is there to hear it, does it make a sound? So, if a pope utters a message in Rome and few local bishops implement these statements with their flocks, does it make a difference? This book argues that the answer to that question is yes, but also that it is contingent upon the initiative of individual American Catholics to take up Pope Francis's challenge. This group includes, but is in no way limited to, bishops. In fact, no Catholic bishop features prominently in these pages. When Francis thought of four "great" Americans, no bishop came to his mind. Perhaps that is not terribly surprising. And yet, it would be defeatist to say that bishops cannot serve as models to U.S. Catholics. The pages of the book will occasionally mention some, as they relate to or complement the figures in question. Sometimes, the relationship will be positive, and other times, the bishop will serve as a cautionary tale on how *not* to interact with a prophetic figure. As John Gehring wittily observes, "Pope Francis has a shepherd's staff, not a magic wand. Even the spiritual leader of more than a billion Catholics can't turn the ocean liner that is the global Catholic Church on his own."[8]

What binds together Pope Francis with the four Americans he mentioned in his congressional address? Each of these figures— Abraham Lincoln, Martin Luther King Jr., Dorothy Day, and Thomas Merton—shares a prophetic stance in the society in which they lived. The present volume will argue that this prophetic stance guided these four figures, guides Francis himself, and has guided any number of other "great" Americans. In these pages, I will attempt to identify various components of the lives of these four figures, as well as identify other such figures to whom we can look today for inspiration. Moreover, Pope Francis will be a critical part of this project, as it is his address and interpretive lens that have proposed the idea of a papally defined "great American." Francis himself is a prophetic figure in the Church, and is an individual that has, at times, been seen in contradistinction to the American ethos. When Francis made his apostolic pilgrimage to the United States in 2015, it was his first visit to the country. It was abundantly clear in those days that his manner of proceeding was markedly different from a number of his brothers in the episcopacy in his host country.

Before describing the role of the prophet in the Church, it would be helpful to distinguish it from its alter ego, the culture warrior.[9] Both terms denote political rhetoric because all rhetoric that involves the *polis* is, by its very nature, political. However, culture warfare is particularly concerned with partisanship. The culture warrior is always interested in making a claim that directly impacts this or that election or matter of public policy. While the prophet may, in fact, be interested in changing or amending a matter of policy, she is not speaking purely as a partisan figure. Rather, the prophet uses her speech to rouse the hearts and minds of her audience, aiming at something deeper and more consequential than the results of the next election. During the same 2015 pilgrimage in which Francis delivered the congressional address that gave the impetus to these pages, he also specifically addressed another group of individuals: the U.S. Catholic bishops, who gathered at St. Matthew's Cathedral in Washington, D.C. During this address, Francis made abundantly clear what he thought about culture warfare: "Harsh and divisive language does not befit the tongue of a pastor, it has no place in his heart; although it may momentarily seem to win the day, only the enduring allure of goodness and love remains truly convincing."[10]

Pope Francis has often recounted that time is greater than space. He discusses this phenomenon in his programmatic apostolic exhortation *Evangelii Gaudium*: "One of the faults which we occasionally observe in sociopolitical activity is that spaces and power are preferred to time and processes" (no. 223). Francis makes a clear distinction between those who prioritize one over the other: "Giving priority to space means madly attempting to keep everything together in the present, trying to possess all the spaces of power and of self-assertion; it is to crystallize processes and presume to hold them back. Giving priority to time means being concerned about initiating processes rather than possessing spaces" (no. 223). Culture warriors are much more interested in prioritizing space, whereas prophets are always eager to put the emphasis on time. The former are generally concerned with positions of power and authority, while the latter are more interested in long-term effects of a timeless message. When bishops and priests, who are meant to radiate the "odour of the sheep,"[11] instead reek of the nearest politician or super PAC, it is particularly odious. Francis is obviously calling for Americans who are willing to be prophets rather than culture warriors. But what is a prophet?

Chapter Outline

This book, because it was inspired by Pope Francis's historic congressional address in September 2015, follows an outline offered by

Francis himself. In choosing the four "great Americans," Francis has shaped my thinking in a quite profound way. Therefore, after dealing with the role of a prophet in the introduction, the first four chapters of this text will turn to the figures whom Francis considers in his address: Lincoln, King, Day, and Merton. However, the reader will quickly notice that these chapters are not biographical sketches of the four figures whom Francis cites, nor do I limit my analysis only to the few lines of Francis's text devoted to each figure. So, what direction do I take in these pages? I begin by linking each figure to key aspects of Francis's pontificate. In so doing, I try to answer the question of why Francis chose the four figures he did. How did they fulfill the role of prophetic figure in the United States in the way that Francis has prescribed for Christians (and all people) throughout the years of his papacy?

In the first chapter, I examine the least likely of the figures whom Francis mentioned, Abraham Lincoln. I say "least likely" because he is the only figure who did not have an explicitly theological formation or outlook in his life, writings, and speeches. This is ironic, though, because he is the figure about whom most Americans know the most biographical information. But why did Francis select him? The chapter focusing on Lincoln considers his role as the "guardian of liberty." What role does theology play in the Emancipation Proclamation? I argue that Lincoln was a precursor to modern Catholic social teaching, as his presidency preceded by three decades the first social encyclical in the modern period. I also examine the timeless question of the public role of Catholics today.[12]

In the next chapter, I consider the other non-Catholic who Francis names in this address: Martin Luther King Jr. Like Lincoln, King is a man about whom most Americans know at least something, if not a great deal. Unlike Lincoln, the grounding of King's life and work was theological and based in faith. Professionally trained in theological studies, King had a different approach than did Lincoln (or, indeed, any of the other three figures). Moreover, King did not serve in elected office. The chapter deals with the civil rights movement as King led it and frames a key connection to the Black Lives Matter movement today. I then turn to King in light of Jesus's commandment to love our neighbor as ourselves. Finally, I propose that King can serve today as a key figure in the creation of an antiracist Church. In so doing, I propose the full integration of the Black Lives Matter movement into the Church today.

The third chapter marks the turn to the first of the two Catholics who Francis offers in his address: Dorothy Day, the cofounder of the Catholic Worker movement. The chapter explores Day's writings on labor and how her prophetic stance overlaps with Francis's own writings. Why is meaningful work actually meaningful at all? Labor, however, is not the only area on which she might be a beacon for Francis. I also argue that Day provides a basic groundwork for Francis's writings and actions in the area of care for creation in the world today. The groundbreaking social encyclical *Laudato Si'* was another way of reading some key themes in Day's own work from decades earlier, just as it was a way of rereading St. Francis of Assisi from centuries earlier. The chapter closes by examining Day and Pope Francis on the issue of nonviolence. The practice of nonviolence was (and remains) at the very heart of the Catholic Worker movement. Francis has also written in this area, especially in his 2020 social encyclical *Fratelli Tutti*. Is there still room for him to be even more prophetic on this front?

Next, I consider Thomas Merton, who, along with Day, was one of the most important twentieth-century Catholic writers in the United States. His groundbreaking autobiography, *The Seven Storey Mountain*, is a classic conversion story. In that account, which Francis cited in front of Congress, Merton writes the words "Loving God, yet hating him." What did these words mean to Merton? What do they mean to Pope Francis? What ought they mean for us today in the twenty-first century? Next, I will ask what it means to consider Merton as a *pontifex*, which is also one of the names a pope takes. Literally, it means "bridge builder." How can one be such a person today, whether or not that person is the pope? Even though Merton was a Trappist monk, he appeals to a popular Jesuit ideal: contemplation in action. What does it mean to be a contemplative in action today? How can we be people of prayer and also people of action?

Even though Francis only names these four Americans explicitly, so many other figures could have been highlighted in this address. The fifth chapter seeks to fill out a fuller list of great Americans whose witness and work seem consistent with the specific examples Francis does offer. In these pages, I present nine women to add to the four mentioned above. Unlike the four individuals Francis selected, most of the nine highlighted in this penultimate chapter are presently living. The chapter considers figures who impact the United States from a variety of different perspectives. I examine three women who have used their ministry as religious sisters in the Catholic Church to impact the national dialogue on the following matters: the death penalty, immigration, and the consistent ethic of life. In a second section, I mention four women who have used their talents in activism to change the trajectory of American history in this century. Finally, I consider two women from the academy who have shaped a good deal of instruction and debate about the presence of God in the world over these last years, and whose influence will be felt for years to come.

The final chapter of the book does something more deliberately than the preceding chapters: ask the question, "What next?" This book presents a great many ideas about the thinking of Pope Francis, as well as the interlocutors he has chosen for himself, and the ones I propose adding to the list. Nevertheless, the emphasis of the book is not to be one of ideas only. Rather, these pages are meant to help us all reflect on how we can be prophets in the Church and the world today. Or, in the words of Pope Francis, we need to bring about a "bold cultural revolution" (*Laudato Si'* 114). I argue that, in order to do this, we first need to find our own models. I challenge us all to begin naming people who can serve as models for us in bringing about a fundamental change to our attitudes and ways of living. Once we have these models, the question then turns to acting in concrete ways to bring about a renewed Church and society. One of the reasons Francis was elected pope in the first place was to reform the curia. While we do not have the authority to do this, the baptized do have the authority to call for crucial changes and reforms. Finally, I consider the prospect of ourselves becoming "great Americans." In what context must we ask that question and carry out a self-examination? I attempt a few answers to these questions.

ACKNOWLEDGMENTS

In the days leading up to Francis's Address to Congress, I had the privilege of serving as an analyst for the coverage of the papal pilgrimage to the United States for *Fox News Radio* and *Fios1 NewYork/New Jersey*. As such, I was able to study the texts of that remarkable week in great detail. As it happened, that congressional address was the only one for which I was "off duty," since I was teaching that day at Fairfield University. In between classes, I was able to attend a viewing party with many students. Upon hearing the four names Francis mentioned, I promised my pupils they would be hearing much more about them later that day. I couldn't get my mind off the address; I still can't. In my heart, I hoped a project like this might emerge. And yet, I very clearly recall the faces of many of those students. They had been etched upon my heart even before I had them in class, and certainly now that years have gone by. As one of my professors once remarked, "The reason I didn't quit graduate school when I was walking to the library in Chicago when it was twenty degrees below zero was because of my students. They would make it worth it." What phenomenal advice. I love my students very dearly, and they make my job everything I dreamed it would be. I thank them for their passion and their presence in my classroom and office.

Some of the material in these pages I have been invited to deliver (in various forms) at wonderful venues, mostly virtual due to the COVID pandemic. I gratefully thank those who invited me, as well as all those who attended the sessions and asked questions that sharpened my argument. In particular, I am grateful to those who attended the presentation of my paper at the 2021 Catholic Theological Society of America Annual Convention, and especially my fellow panelist, Brent

Little, who is a wonderful friend and always my first sounding board for ecclesial matters. We sat at lunch the day after Pope Francis was elected and prayed that we would get "five good years" out of him. We are happy that we undershot that one! Earlier in 2021, Brent and I were part of a panel organized by the Loyola University Chicago's Hank Center for the Catholic Intellectual Heritage. We were joined by our friend and colleague Karen Ross, who is an expert on the topic of chapter 5 of this book and is always ready to share her insights and expertise for my edification and enjoyment, as well as for the improvement of my research. That panel, when I first offered a broad overview of this study, was organized by Mike Murphy, Meghan Twomey, and Kathleen McNutt.

When I wrote this volume, I was happily employed in the Philosophy and Religious Studies department at Marywood University, where I had generous colleagues who supported me and my work on this book. In a particular way, I thank the very capable department chair, Sarah Kenehan, who is now a colleague at the University of Scranton. As I edit these words, I am about to embark on a new role at the University of Scranton, where it will be my privilege to devote my time to the mission and ministry of that wonderful community. I thank Rev. Joe Marina, SJ, for the confidence he has shown in me. In a particular way, I am so thankful to very close friends who put up with my running commentary on this subject for years, and often grounded me when my writing stress or research obsession grew beyond a healthy size: Joe Blankenship, Brendan Coffey, SJ, and Mike Goode in very frequent phone calls; and Sarah Farrell, Gigi Herrmann, Jim Keane, and Maggie Wells in frequent Zoom meetings. In addition to the theologians mentioned above, I also relied on insights from Kevin Ahern, Christian Cintron, and Michael Petrin.

I wish to thank the President and Publisher of Paulist Press, Rev. Mark-David Janus, CSP, for inviting me to consider this project. From the very first contact, he has been unfailingly gracious with his advice and encouragement. Likewise, the Editorial Director, Paul McMahon, has been very helpful, and the Senior Academic Editor, Donna Crilly, has been invaluable in getting this to press. I am grateful to everyone at Paulist for making this possible. This book would not have gotten to this stage without two friends and colleagues who read every word of it, caught many errors, and pushed me to improve it: Eric Martin and Rev. Terrence Moran. They have both been friends for many years and have

Acknowledgments

an eye for details that has helped me so much in the writing of these pages. More significantly, though, their example in life has been of the greatest importance to me. They are both faithful people whose lives show fidelity that I hope to emulate in some small way. Thank you so much for putting your stamps of wit, eloquence, and precision on these pages.

My final words of thanks go to my family. As always, my parents have been constantly checking on the progress of this book, and their love and support of me has never reached any limitations. Every day my daughter Samantha has asked me, "Daddy, did you write your Pope Francis book today?" In a recent Zoom presentation I delivered, she watched and wondered aloud every time I mentioned "Francis," whether I meant the saint or the pope. That alone gave me more joy than any complete manuscript ever could! Finally, I dedicate these pages to my wife, Julia Cosacchi. As with everything else I have ever written since we met in 2009, she read every word of this project and commented on it; she also compiled the index. More than a copyeditor, however, she makes sure that our common life together is ordered in such a way that things continue to run smoothly and faithfully, with an eye toward what matters most. Obviously, "thank you" doesn't even begin to cover it. Nevertheless, this book would simply not have been possible without her, so it is the least I can offer.

I have written these words on a particularly apt day. Throughout the pages of this book, I refer to conversion time and again. Today happens to commemorate not only the most significant conversion in Christianity, but also the patronal feast of the Paulist Fathers, whose congregation is responsible both for publishing this work and for so much good done in the Church. Because of the new position I now have, I revised them on another day with great meaning to me, because it represents the faith community to which we once belonged and which we often visit on trips to Connecticut. Some of the best preaching I have ever heard was delivered in that sanctuary, and I am grateful for my affiliation with those people of great faith at the Parish of Saint Anthony.

January 25, 2022
Feast of the Conversion of Saint Paul the Apostle

June 13, 2022
Feast of Saint Anthony of Padua
Scranton

INTRODUCTION

A Prophetic Papacy

Prophecy: What It Is and What It Isn't

In this introduction, I will address five interrelated tasks. First, I will try to answer the question, What is prophecy? Second, I will respond to the question, Who were the prophets? In a third section, I will elaborate the social location of a few of the prophets and suggest why that is important context to consider. Fourth, I will address another question: What can we learn from the prophets today? Fifth, and finally, I will consider what the prophetic tradition in the Church might be.

What Is Prophecy?

When teaching my students about the prophets, I try to make the course material as concrete as possible by asking precise questions and trying to identify precise answers. Of course, I tell them that the word *prophet* comes from the Greek word *pro-phates*, which means "to foresee" or "one who speaks on behalf of another." In Hebrew, the word by which prophets called themselves was *nabi*, which literally means "one called" or "one who is called."[1] I invite my students to define *prophet* themselves, and offer for their consideration the definition I have found to be most apt: "the person who pays attention to the silent voices."[2]

1

A key distinction is often suggested by a very wise scholar of the Hebrew Scriptures, Richard Clifford, SJ: we need to discern between false prophets and true prophets.[3] There are two basic criteria in order to be a true prophet according to the Book of Deuteronomy. The first criterion is whether or not the prophet's prophecy comes true. If the prophet warns about the future and those warnings never come to pass, then we are talking about a false prophet. Second, as Clifford puts it, "did the prophet's teaching agree with the faith of the fathers, with the main tenets of Yahwistic belief, or did it lead the people to abandon the one God for the seductive gods of their pagan neighbors?"[4] It is not always abundantly clear if a prophet is speaking for God or if they are speaking for themselves alone. But true biblical prophets, as Sister Margaret Farley, RSM, notes, "were individuals who were called and commissioned by God, usually to deliver a message to God's people."[5] But again, not every person who seems to be a prophet is an authentic one.

This is sort of low-hanging fruit for us today, but I would suggest to you that many people who, at least ostensibly, claim the prophetic tradition as an important part of their own tradition, have also claimed former president Donald Trump as a type of prophet. Even though I obviously wish I were kidding, it is instructive to watch the news occasionally when a reporter will do a type of focus group with mostly white, Evangelical Christians and ask them why they support President Trump. Almost invariably, some of the number will answer that they support Trump because of divine mandate. They will say explicitly that they believe the president has been chosen by God to have the position he currently holds. There is never any follow-up as to whether they believe Joe Biden, Barack Obama, or Bill Clinton was also chosen by God, but I am always curious to know their answer. In any case, we can see that certain false prophets, whose message is not God's message, always have some sort of following. But, in any case, not all prophets are popular. Notice that popularity is not one of the criteria for authentic prophecy. Let's turn, then, to some of the prophets and examine their messages.

Who Were the Prophets?

The books of the Hebrew Scriptures, commonly referred to as the Old Testament, are broken up into three broad categories: First, Torah, which comprises the first five books of the Bible; second, Writings; and third, Prophets, which in addition to the fifteen prophets also include Joshua, Judges, the two Books of Samuel, and the two Books of Kings.[6] In this section, I will briefly introduce the fifteen prophetic books most commonly associated with prophecy in the Hebrew Scriptures. The first mistake we could make in discussing these figures is to think they all were the same types of people. There are four different titles used for these fifteen figures in the Hebrew Scriptures: *seer*, *diviner* (someone who is able to communicate with the world of the sacred in order to discover information that will be useful to those who consult him), *man of God*, and *prophet*.[7] In other words, if you've seen one prophet, you've only seen one prophet. No two are necessarily cut from similar cloth. That point notwithstanding, there are certainly some areas of overlap and some common motifs that some of the prophets share.

As I have already indicated, the list of fifteen prophets most commonly described as such in the Hebrew Scriptures does not even come close to accounting for all of the figures that Jews consider prophetic. Among the fifteen, three are the most easily recognizable: Isaiah, Jeremiah, and Ezekiel. As scripture scholar Joseph Blenkinsopp notes, "According to a rabbinic dictum there were forty-eight prophets and seven prophetesses in Israel, a conclusion no doubt based on a head count over the entire Hebrew Bible."[8] The prophets that we generally think of in the Bible could already look back on a long history with God in Israel.[9] As Gerhard von Rad explains in a very readable survey of the prophetic books of the Bible entitled *The Message of the Prophets*, there are four features that bring about the work of the prophets: first, the degeneracy of Yahwism because of syncretism, or the merging of different religions. Second, Israel had "disregarded Yahweh's guiding hand and had become politically autonomous." Third, there was a major economic and social shift, whereby taxation and civil service had disintegrated the old social order, giving the landowners a tremendous amount of control over the vast majority of the people. Social injustice ensued. The fourth development was a shift in the political power of the time—namely, the rise of Assyria as a kingdom—which was accompanied by a constant threat to Palestine beginning in the eighth century.[10]

Back to the list of prophets. In addition to the three I mentioned above, there is the "Book of the Twelve," comprising Hosea, Joel, Amos, Obadiah, Jonah, Micah, Nahum, Habakkuk, Zephaniah, Haggai,

Zechariah, and Malachi. I will cite from just a few. The first example of the calling of a prophet I present here may be familiar to many readers, especially practicing Catholics who will recognize this from a very popular hymn, citing Isaiah:

> In the year that King Uzziah died [738 BCE], I saw the Lord sitting on a throne, high and lofty; and the hem of his robe filled the temple. Seraphs were in attendance above him; each had six wings: with two they covered their faces, and with two they covered their feet, and with two they flew. And one called to another and said:
>
> "Holy, holy, holy is the LORD of hosts;
> the whole earth is full of his glory."
>
> The pivots on the thresholds shook at the voices of those who called, and the house filled with smoke. And I said: "Woe is me! I am lost, for I am a man of unclean lips, and I live among a people of unclean lips; yet my eyes have seen the King, the LORD of hosts!"
> Then one of the seraphs flew to me, holding a living coal that had been taken from the altar with a pair of tongs. The seraph touched my mouth with it and said: "Now that this has touched your lips, your guilt has departed and your sin is blotted out." Then I heard the voice of the Lord saying, "Whom shall I send, and who will go for us?" And I said "Here am I; send me!" (Isaiah 6:1–8)[11]

Father Daniel Berrigan, SJ, no stranger to modern prophecy himself, writes, "We are granted no inkling of Isaiah's life prior to his vision. It is as though to his own eyes nothing worth recording happened prior to the summons. Here and in the subsequent oracles is no hint that a conversion of note preceded the vision. He cries out a confession of sin. But this would seem to imply nothing more than sages and saints have known through the ages—the holiness of God casts into shadow everything human, including our presumed virtue."[12] In other words, we need not be put off by our own weakness and failing, because we all surely have them. We need not be ashamed of our sins; like Isaiah and Berrigan, we are sinners. We need not think that we must have out-of-body mystical experiences of the Lord of hosts sitting on a throne. None of these things is necessary to be a prophet. Simply being called, which we all are, is necessary. Simply paying attention to the silent voices is necessary. But where did they come from, and why did they speak?

Social Condition of (Some of) the Prophets

Since I mentioned above that not all the prophets were the same, not all of them had the same approach, not all of them spoke precisely the same way, and certainly not all of them lived as precise contemporaries, it goes without saying that there does not exist a one-size-fits-all approach to understanding the social setting of these prophets. Therefore, I will select a few to examine now.[13] But all fifteen of these prophets have a disturbing and consistent message: the end has come or is very imminent for Israel. The traditions of assurance no longer held true in each case.

Amos is among the earliest of these fifteen prophets chronologically.[14] Based on the text, we can date Amos in the middle of the eighth century BCE, since he was active during the reigns of King Uzziah of Judah (783–742) and King Jeroboam II of Israel (786–746). He is a native of the Southern Kingdom, Judah, and travels to the Northern Kingdom, Israel, to proclaim the word of God.[15] One of the key issues of social injustice that many of the prophets focus on are conditions that lead to widespread poverty among the people. As J. David Pleins notes, "With Amos we obtain our first insight into the plight of the poor in the biblical world: The poor are 'at mercy of the arbitrary expectations and demands of the rich.'"[16] In Amos's time and place, we see the consequences of a system that had spread and grown in practice: debt slavery. In this practice, many people were sold into service because they had no way to stay out of debt. This enslavement was a way to pay off their debts. As Amos describes the situation,

> Thus says the LORD [notice here that God is speaking through
>   the mouth of the prophet]:
> For three transgressions of Israel,
>   and for four, I will not revoke the punishment;
> because they sell the righteous for silver,
>   and the needy for a pair of sandals—

they who trample the head of the poor into the dust of the earth,
  and push the afflicted out of the way…
so that my holy name is profaned. (Amos 2:6–7)

Amos goes on in this vein and declares promises of very bad things on the horizon from God's hands.

The point is clear in the Book of Amos. In the face of so much injustice that is taking place in Israel, the prophet is making it abundantly clear that God takes note of the various ways the rich are causing further suffering on the already impoverished. And time and time again, Amos reminds these rich people that God will judge them harshly for their ways. As Pleins contends, "To the prophet, the maintenance of a high standard of living through exploitative structures and activities constituted a rejection of the community's obligations to YHWH."[17] But notice one major attribute of Amos's writings here: there is no real sense that the prophet is calling for the people to overthrow the state.[18] What Amos is definitely after is for the people to undergo a communal conversion experience whereby they return to the Lord:

Seek good and not evil,
  that you may live;
and so the LORD, the God of hosts, will be with you,
  just as you have said.
Hate evil and love good,
  and establish justice in the gate;
it may be that the LORD, the God of hosts,
  will be gracious to the remnant of Joseph. (Amos 5:14–15)

Of the fifteen prophets, only Jonah is reported to have fled, even though it is likely that Jeremiah wanted to do the same. Jonah is the quintessential example of a prophet who preached the suffering, death, and resurrection of the nation. Most casual readers, I am guessing, would quickly recall Jonah's entrapment in the belly of a fish. This is the perfect time to pause for station identification. The Book of Jonah, which is a short story about Jonah's journeys with God and the people of Nineveh rather than a series of oracles and preaching from Jonah, makes it the odd book out of the Book of Twelve.[19] Jonah's journey is not meant to be read as literally true.[20] Of course, as I am constantly reminding my students, that fact does not mean that it holds no meaning for us. There is great meaning in the Book of Jonah.

The reason Jonah appeals to me is that his actions in response to God are precisely the same ones that I often find in myself. After he is called, the story goes like this: "But Jonah set out to flee to Tarshish from the presence of the LORD. He went down to Joppa and found a ship going to Tarshish; so he paid his fare and went on board, to go with them to Tarshish, away from the presence of the LORD" (1:3). Sometimes, we may feel called to do something and for one reason or another think that it can't possibly be the right thing. Jonah decides to flee because he is confident of God's mercy, and he doesn't think the Ninevites are worthy of it. The earliest readers of the Book of Jonah would have already known that Nineveh was wiped out. The book is written at some point after the year 539 BCE, after the exile. Nineveh is destroyed in 612 and Jerusalem in 587. The social injustice of which the Ninevites are guilty is the reason their destruction comes about. And yet, God's mercy can overcome even those terrible deeds. That is the constant struggle of our prophets. On the one hand, they must preach the truth of God's justice and the importance of upholding that divine justice at all times; on the other hand, they must always be cognizant that God's mercy is always greater than our sense of what is fitting.

What Can We Learn from the Prophets Today?

Can we learn anything from the prophets today? Pope Francis's invocation of four great Americans as prophetic gives us a resounding answer in the affirmative. If the prophets are not trying to overthrow the state, what are they trying to do? They are trying to lift up the poor and turn all of our minds to God. The prophet Micah, while active in the last quarter of the eighth century, was based in the Southern Kingdom of Judah, as opposed to Amos's station in Israel. Even though there are passages of impending doom in Micah's writing, it does not seem to be as omnipresent as it is in Amos's prophecy. And even while Amos is clearly open to the final hope that is possible with the Lord, Micah emphasizes it a bit more.

Another prophetic area prominent for Micah is the emphasis on nonviolence.[21] He is upfront on the great importance of being people of integrity who enact justice at all times, always in obedience to God's law. After posing some rhetorical questions of whether God will be pleased with all the sacrificial offerings of the people, Micah professes,

> He has told you, O mortal, what is good;
>   and what does the LORD require of you
> but to do justice, and to love kindness,
>   and to walk humbly with your God? (6:8)

We already know that sacrifice without justice is abominable to the Lord. Listen to another accusation Micah makes against the rich:

> Your wealthy are full of violence;
>   your inhabitants speak lies,
>   with tongues of deceit in their mouths. (6:12)

And what is the result of all this violence? Micah's verdict: "Therefore I have begun to strike you down, making you desolate because of your sins" (6:13).

But Micah's most overt disavowal of violence comes in 4:1–5. The first three verses are basically identical to an oracle that also appears in the second chapter of Isaiah, but I cite Micah here:

> In days to come
>   the mountain of the LORD's house
> shall be established as the highest of the mountains,
>   and shall be raised up above the hills.
> Peoples shall stream to it,
>   and many nations shall come and say:
> "Come, let us go up to the mountain of the LORD,
>   to the house of the God of Jacob;
> that he may teach us his ways
>   and that we may walk in his paths."
> For from out of Zion shall go forth instruction,
>   and the word of the LORD from Jerusalem.
> He shall judge between many peoples,
>   and shall arbitrate between strong nations far away;

they shall beat their swords into plowshares,
    and their spears into pruning hooks;
nation shall not lift sword against nation,
    neither shall they learn war any more;
but they shall all sit under their own vines and under their own
      fig trees,
    and no one shall make them afraid;
    for the mouth of the LORD of hosts has spoken.
For all the peoples walk,
    each in the name of its god,
but we will walk in the name of the LORD our God
    forever and ever. (4:1–5)[22]

What about the prophetic example of Jesus? Pope Francis would certainly profess that Jesus is more than a prophet only. As Jesus himself once said, "Something greater than Jonah is here" (Matt 12:41). And indeed, there is. However, we would also be ignorant of Jesus and his way of life if we did not readily admit that he revered the prophetic texts. Recall that his own inaugural address was citing directly from Isaiah's prophecy:

The Spirit of the Lord is upon me,
    because he has anointed me
      to bring good news to the poor.
He has sent me to proclaim release to the captives
    and recovery of sight to the blind,
      to let the oppressed go free,
to proclaim the year of the Lord's favor. (Luke 4:18–19)

St. Luke continues by illustrating what the congregation thought of that performance: "The eyes of all in the synagogue were fixed on him" (4:20). They were so transfixed in part because Jesus omits the very next line of Isaiah's prophecy from the sixty-first chapter of that book, which reads, "and the day of vengeance of our God" (Isa 61:2b).[23] Jesus's preaching of God's kingdom has nothing to do with vengeance or violence. Rather, he embraces the nonviolence of Micah, chapter 4.

In his classic work *Jesus of Nazareth: What He Wanted, Who He Was*, Gerhard Lohfink reminds us that in the prophetic tradition in which Jesus teaches, preaches, worships, and prays, he follows a path whereby "the prophets have the vision of an Israel that, by its example, teaches the nations how people can live together in peace and without violence."[24] Jesus takes the emphasis on nonviolence even one step further with an absolute prohibition of violence throughout his teaching. And it has tremendous consequences. The most important consequence for us today is that the teachings of nonviolence are not some sort of naïve instruction meant only for Jesus. Violence is antithetical to God's kingdom. Furthermore, nonviolence is not something that will only be enacted in the end times. In the parallel passage in Isaiah to the Mican passage I just cited, the prophet ends with these words:

> O house of Jacob,
>   come, let us walk
>   in the light of the LORD! (Isa 2:5)

In other words, he does not say, "Let us light a lamp so as to simulate the light of the Lord"; nor does he say, "Let us think about what it will be like to walk in the way of the Lord." No, Isaiah makes it clear that this is a path that can be trod right now, by all of us. In the Church, there is already a path that has been paved in the tradition by many prophets. It is to the Church, the people of God, that I now turn.

What Is the Prophetic Tradition in the Church?

Some forty years ago, Walter Brueggemann wrote these words in his book *The Prophetic Imagination*: "The contemporary American church is so largely enculturated to the American ethos of consumerism that it has little power to believe or act."[25] These words still ring true today. As I have tried to make clear in this section, Brueggemann's description is precisely the line of thinking that the prophets dealt with millennia ago in Israel and Judah. In other words, the ethos of consumerism that Brueggemann lamented forty years ago and that we could well lament today is not peculiar only to the United States in the late twentieth and early twenty-first centuries. It is the ethos that embodies the empire. It was the same ethos that Jesus prophesied against some two thousand years ago, and against which the early Church witnessed with their own prophetic message shortly after Jesus's death and resurrection.

The response to the prophets in each of those historical time periods was similar: the prophets suffered because of their unpopularity.

To be clear, not every prophet suffers the same way, and many of these prophets do have reasonable followings too. But there always seems to be some influential group that wants them to fail. Depending upon how influential that group is, and how much the evil spirit has taken hold of them, the results can be fatal. Think, for example, of one of the most prophetic Catholic bishops of the last century: Óscar Romero, who was canonized a saint by Pope Francis in 2018. St. Romero was shot and killed while celebrating the Eucharist on March 24, 1980. The day before, during his Sunday homily, he preached these words, at the very end of a homily that lasted nearly two hours:

> I would like to appeal in a special way to the army's enlisted men, and in particular to the ranks of the *Guardia Nacional* and the police—those in the barracks. Brothers: you are part of our own people. You kill your own *campesino* brothers and sisters. Before an order to kill that a man may give, God's law must prevail: *Thou shalt not kill!* No soldier is obliged to obey an order against the law of God. No one has to fulfill an immoral law. It is time to take back your consciences and to obey your consciences rather than the orders of sin. The Church, defender of the rights of God, of the law of God, of human dignity, of the person, cannot remain silent before such abominations. We want the government to understand seriously that reforms are worth nothing if they are stained with so much blood. In the name of God, and in the name of this suffering people, whose laments rise to heaven each day more tumultuous, I beg you, I beseech you, I order you in the name of God: Stop the repression![26]

This prophetic discourse had real consequences for Romero. He became a martyr.[27]

Here in the United States, I am reminded of Father Daniel Berrigan, who was a Jesuit for over seventy years. Berrigan's commitment to nonviolence was not part of his DNA. Four of his five brothers served in the military at one point in time; one of Berrigan's earliest poems, published in *America*, was dedicated to his "four soldier brothers."[28] When his brother Philip returned from service in World War II and visited Dan, the brothers participated in great celebrations at the Jesuit seminary where he lived, all the while celebrating the nation's military prowess. This is an incredible thing to imagine because only a few decades later, May 17, 1968, those two brothers, along with seven other Catholics, entered the draft board offices in Catonsville, Maryland, stole hundreds of draft files, and burned them in the parking lot with homemade napalm in order to register their discontent with the Vietnam War.[29] Like Amos, they did not advocate for the overthrow of the state, but they did make it clear that violence against other human beings could never be used justly. In addition to widespread discontent and unpopularity among many Catholics, the Jesuits themselves disparaged Berrigan. Upon his release from federal prison, Berrigan found his belongings removed from his Jesuit residence and placed on the front porch. He was persona non grata among his own confreres.[30]

Is there a legitimate tradition of prophecy in the Church today? There is, and it is so foundational that it appears in the very ritual that welcomes each new Christian into life in the Spirit, and indeed welcomes every new member of the Church. At baptism, the newly reborn Christian is anointed "priest, *prophet*, and king." Not only do we have a right to be prophets in the Church, but we have an obligation by virtue of our baptism. But baptism is not magic. Simply because one is baptized into prophecy does not mean we take on the mantle automatically.

We know that the tradition of prophecy is promoted in the Church in the pages of the New Testament, the Church that immediately practices baptism at the behest of the risen and ascending Christ. Here is a sampling: "At that time prophets came down from Jerusalem to Antioch" (Acts 11:27); "[Philip] had four unmarried daughters who had the gift of prophecy" (Acts 21:9); "Now in the church at Antioch there were prophets and teachers: Barnabas, Simeon who was called Niger, Lucius of Cyrene, Manaen, a member of the court of Herod the ruler, and Saul" (Acts 13:1); "If I have prophetic powers, and understand all mysteries and all knowledge, and if I have faith, so as to move mountains, but do not have love, I am nothing" (1 Cor 13:2); "Pursue love and strive for the spiritual gifts, and especially that you may prophesy" (1 Cor 14:1). And Paul, in his letter to the Romans, lists prophecy among the offices of the

Church alongside teaching, ministry, exhorting, giving, leading, and being compassionate (12:6–8). All of this is simply to say that prophecy is not only bound to the Hebrew Scriptures but is also part of the New Testament and is our heritage in the Church today. Pope Francis reminds us of our heritage by calling our attention to four great Americans. It is to these figures that I now turn.

Chapter One

ABRAHAM LINCOLN AND FREEDOM

The first great man that I talked with in the United States freely, who in no single instance reminded me of the difference between himself and myself, of the difference of color.

—Frederick Douglass[1]

It is likely the case that when most Americans heard Pope Francis's address to Congress, the figure about whom they knew—or at least *thought* they knew—most was Abraham Lincoln, the sixteenth president of the United States (1861–65). But why did Pope Francis shine the spotlight on Lincoln during his address? Since Lincoln was perhaps the greatest politician in American history, the politicians gathered in the room had a better handle on that aspect of Lincoln's life than did the pope. Unlike Dorothy Day and Thomas Merton, Lincoln was not Catholic. Unlike Martin Luther King, it is not obvious if he was motivated by the Christian faith in his life's work.[2] And yet, as Francis noted in his intervention on Lincoln, the principal action of his life was rooted in his Emancipation Proclamation. I examine the relationship of this brief executive order with theology in the first section of this chapter.

In the next section, I turn to Lincoln as a potential precursor to modern Catholic social teaching (CST). It is worth mentioning that the distinction *modern* normally refers to the body of social encyclicals released by popes since Pope Leo XIII's promulgation of *Rerum Novarum* in 1891, thirty-five years after Lincoln's assassination.[3] Of course, it is important to note that while *modern* may be a valuable way to describe what we read from the end of the nineteenth century onward, CST is older and more expansive than what we find only in this more recent timeframe.[4] Therefore, even as Lincoln was governing, Catholic social teaching was being promulgated. Lincoln is hardly ever considered a fundamental figure in CST, yet Pope Francis cites him in this landmark address. Why? Francis mentions three principles of CST that have come to shape the tradition in a profound way: the common good, solidarity, and subsidiarity. In the second section of this chapter, I examine how Lincoln's political career emphasized these key values.

Finally, in the last part of this chapter, I explore the role of Catholics in public life today. I write these words during the first term of the second Roman Catholic president in the history of the United States, Joseph Biden. Biden's own words in his inaugural address, as well as his frequent practice of worshiping at the eucharistic liturgy, make his Catholicism a focal point of his presidency. And yet, there is no shortage of discordance between Biden and the United States Conference of Catholic Bishops.[5] In a statement released on the day of Biden's inauguration as president, Archbishop José Gomez writes these harsh words:

> I must point out that our new President has pledged to pursue certain policies that would advance moral evils and threaten human life and dignity, most seriously in the areas of abortion, contraception, marriage, and gender. Of deep concern is the liberty of the Church and the freedom of believers to live according to their consciences.[6]

Rather than being prophetic, these words take on the harsh and divisive quality of cultural warfare that I alluded to in the preface. Lincoln, in his own life, provided us with the model of a prophetic political leader. How would a politician of his ilk be accepted in the United States today? What can Lincoln teach Catholics wishing to serve in elected office? I take up these questions in the third part of the chapter. For now, though, it is to the Emancipation Proclamation that I turn.

"Guardian of Liberty": The Emancipation Proclamation and Theology

It is a matter of some debate as to which of Lincoln's writings or addresses is his most famous. Among the main contenders would be the Emancipation Proclamation, issued in its final form on January 1, 1863.[7] When Pope Francis refers to Lincoln as "the guardian of liberty," the Emancipation Proclamation is perhaps the text that first came to the minds of the congressional audience as well as the millions watching around the world. But Lincoln's role as the "emancipator" goes beyond the few paragraphs dedicated to him in Francis's address. Moreover, Lincoln is much more complicated and nuanced than the popular imagery of him in our school lectures or national hagiographies. While Lincoln may rightly be considered the guardian of liberty, he also falls short of what Ibram X. Kendi would call an antiracist, or "one who is supporting an antiracist policy through their actions or expressing an antiracist idea."[8] Clearly, the Emancipation Proclamation ushered into American life one of the most antiracist policies ever enacted. And yet Lincoln's own philosophy remains in question. As he wrote to Horace Greeley on August 20, 1862, "If I could save the Union without freeing any slave I would do it, and if I could save it by freeing all the slaves I would do it."[9] Or again, he made his understanding of hierarchy clear: "Inasmuch as they cannot so live, while they do remain together, there must be the position of superior and inferior, and I as much as any other man am in favor of having the superior position assigned to the white race."[10]

So how did Lincoln get from a position that any fair-minded person today would consider repugnant to the status of cherished hero of the Civil War? Indeed, the most influential Black American of the nineteenth century, Frederick Douglass, recalled Lincoln as "the first great man that I talked with in the United States freely, who in no single instance reminded me of the difference between himself and myself, of the difference of color."[11] As Doris Kearns Goodwin astutely notes, this was no trivial statement, because Douglass had had occasion to converse with "dozens of celebrated abolitionists, including Wendell Phillips, William Lloyd Garrison, and Salmon Chase."[12] By naming Lincoln in his address, Francis made an important choice. As with King, Lincoln is an American that everyone listening to the address would know by name and reputation. But what is the theological significance of his guardianship of liberty?

Lincoln would not have been familiar with liberation theology. In fact, it is anachronistic to apply such a term to Lincoln's own time.[13] However, some of the key elements of twentieth-century Latin American liberation theology also apply to the Emancipation Proclamation, and indeed, Lincoln's tenure as president. As Phillip Berryman explains, liberation theology is

1. An interpretation of Christian faith out of the suffering, struggle, and hope of the poor.
2. A critique of society and the ideologies sustaining it.
3. A critique of the activity of the Church and of Christians from the angle of the poor.[14]

It is clear that Lincoln was not working out of a faith context in the same way that liberation theologians were. Nevertheless, there is certainly some overlap in the Emancipation Proclamation that sets it apart as a protoliberation text.

In the key words of the Emancipation Proclamation, Lincoln proclaimed, "All persons held as slaves within any State or designated part of a State, the people whereof shall then be in rebellion against the United States, shall be then, thenceforward, and forever free." As I have already noted above, even as Lincoln issued the Emancipation Proclamation, one should not confuse him with liberation theologians who saw a fundamental equality among all human beings. There is one theme that comes through in Lincoln's words: what Leonardo and Clodovis Boff name "liberated human potential becomes liberative."[15]

To say that Lincoln is the guardian of liberty, as Francis does, is to say that Lincoln is also the guarantor that human beings would be free and would have this liberated potential. Liberated potential takes shape in any variety of ways. It means that people can marry and raise a family, earn a living at a job that they love, spend their free time in ways that are enjoyable, engage in relationships of mutual growth and understanding with friends and family, take part in dialogues with the wider community, and be a member of the larger society. Especially today, in a world that boasts of being a global community, such liberated human potential has even more room to soar. At the same time, we know that many human beings (to say nothing of nonhuman creatures) are not granted this potential. What M. Shawn Copeland said of chattel slavery leading Christianity to a crossroad may well be said of the condition of the Church today vis-à-vis many of the poorest human beings today: "discipleship or duplicity."[16]

As Copeland has reminded us, even if those key words of the Emancipation Proclamation are revolutionary, because they are limited to the seceded states only and not any slaves who were held in the North, they were also "ambiguous."[17] On a few occasions surrounding the promulgation of this act, Lincoln noted that it was God's will that the slaves in the Southern states be freed.[18] Unfortunately, many American Catholic bishops at the time did not see it that way at all.[19]

Even though Lincoln was not perfect, and certainly did not reach the levels of the antiracists of his own day, I propose that Francis was not wrong in calling our attention to him during his address. Properly understanding Lincoln as a force for good and a prophetic figure during his time can help American Catholics understand what discipleship might look like today, as opposed to a more duplicitous way of life. Such duplicity, perhaps, could be seen in Lincoln's own view of slavery, which was different for him as an individual and as a public official. On September 13, 1862, only a few months before the Emancipation Proclamation was issued, Lincoln offered a reply to the Emancipation Memorial presented by a group of Chicago clergy in which he clearly doubted the efficacy of any such proclamation as he would soon draft and enact in the coming weeks and months: "Would my *word* free the slaves, when I cannot even enforce the Constitution in rebel states?"[20] Steering clear of duplicity is part of the Christian life, but it also raises important questions when it comes to those in the public square. Is it possible for such elected officials to avoid duplicity at all times? When it comes to duplicity, can good fruit come from a bad tree?

In Lincoln's case, few people today would agree with his official stance as it was illuminated above; few would contend that slavery was acceptable if it would save the Union, even if that was not his personal belief. And yet, it is also unconvincing to say that Lincoln was not a liberator for Black people in what was the Confederacy. What would have happened to chattel slavery had Lincoln never been elected and the United States was left with any of the unsuccessful contenders for the presidency?[21] This is an uncomfortable question because it raises the tension of political realism for elected officials. When the Boffs discuss the liberation of human beings in society, they grapple with the reality of social sin and remark that in order to bring about this liberated humanity, a social conversion is necessary: "This social conversion is brought about through transformative social struggle, with the tactics and strategy suited to bringing about the changes needed. Social sin has to be opposed by social grace, fruit of God's gift and of human endeavor inspired by God."[22] Lincoln saw the social sin of chattel slavery at work, and he understood, even if he was not an outwardly religious man, that God's grace was what would bring about the social change necessary to put the country on a different course. In so doing, he was a politician whose Emancipation Proclamation presaged the idea of liberation that would inform liberation theology.[23] The same could be said for his relationship with a nascent movement of social teaching in the Catholic Church.

Lincoln as Precursor to Modern Catholic Social Teaching

When Pope Leo XIII promulgated *Rerum Novarum* on May 15, 1891, he was already working with a long tradition of Catholic teaching on social questions. Even though the birth of Catholic social thought is usually dated to these waning days of the nineteenth century, many of the themes with which Leo dealt were already part of the Catholic understanding of society. Therefore, Lincoln merits further attention when considering the development of Catholic social teaching.[24] First, the Catholic position on slavery is of the highest importance when painting the image of Lincoln as the guardian of liberty.

In the spring semester of 2021, during the COVID pandemic that rocked the entire world, including the classrooms of colleges and universities everywhere, I found myself teaching a course that I had recently developed: Racism and the Church. The class comprised thirteen honors-level students, only one of whom was a person of color. I, the instructor, am also white. We were dealing with many uncomfortable topics in that course, which was a grace beyond telling, at least for me! Nevertheless, not all of the moments of discomfort resulted in universal agreement. One such occasion will always remain with me. During the third session of the course, one of my students raised her hand and shared that she had been discussing the previous week's reading with a friend in the student cafeteria over supper the previous evening. My pride that our course had escaped the walls of the classroom or library soon mixed with horror at learning what happened next to my student. "All of a sudden," she reported, her voice quavering, "a guy came over to our table, slammed his fist down and yelled, 'The Church is not racist.' We lost our appetite if you know what I mean." This was an apropos turn of phrase because it reflected a truth among white American Catholics: there is no appetite for hearing about our Church's racist past, and even less to discuss its racist present.

One of the most common misperceptions about the Catholic Church is that its teachings never change.[25] Understanding the development of the tradition, however, can lead us down the path of understanding how the Church has dealt with slavery. Owning other human beings as slaves was not always considered a sin in the Catholic Church. In fact, it was so much a part of the norm that even popes owned slaves.[26] However, it was the Holy See that spoke in defense of the rights of Black people in contrast to the practice of chattel slavery that was so much a part of American and American Catholic history. In his 1839 apostolic letter, *In Supremo Apostolatus Fastigio*, Pope Gregory XVI condemned the slave trade. As Cyprian Davis writes of Gregory, "Both as cardinal and later as pope, he had a keen interest in missions and in the problems facing missionaries. This experience gave him firsthand knowledge of the depredations of the slave trade. Faced with what he considered an evil, he was intransigent in condemning it."[27] Nevertheless, in the United States, there was a mixed reaction to Gregory's proclamation. It is not a uniquely American phenomenon for Catholic bishops to challenge the teachings of the pope, so this was not an isolated incident. During Pope Francis's pontificate, many U.S. bishops have battled the pope's own message.[28] Two centuries earlier, Davis notes, the situation was similar: "The attitude of Catholics in the United States was somewhat different [than Gregory's]. Many bishops were slaveowners. Inevitably some of them did engage in the buying and selling of slaves, just as many priests and religious did."[29] Bishop John England, one of the leading Catholic prelates of the South, openly dissented from Gregory's teaching, but did so by spinning the words of the pope and claiming that a private conversation with Gregory in Rome gave Americans permission to own slaves.[30]

What does Catholic social teaching say today about slavery? The teaching is clear: slavery is listed among the gravest evils that can be employed in the world today. As the fathers of Vatican II write, slavery ranks alongside deportation and arbitrary imprisonment as "insults to human dignity" (*Gaudium et Spes* 27).[31] Along with a wide-ranging catalogue of other sins, the Council considers slavery morally grave. Vatican II was a watershed moment on the Catholic teaching on slavery, as it was in so many other areas of Church life. As a number of scholars have pointed out, even by the mid-twentieth century there was "no text by which the Church or any pope condemned slavery outright or proclaimed its intrinsic evil."[32] Again, there was no ecclesial appetite to deal with the Church's complicity in antebellum racism, and certainly no magisterial stomach to address the Church's slaveholding past.

This is where Francis's "great" American, Lincoln, fits into the tale. Like the Catholic Church, Lincoln did not come to an abolitionist (or at least emancipationist) stance overnight. And among Catholics, in fact, there was only measured support for Lincoln as a presidential candidate and later for his issuance of the proclamation itself.[33] But for his own part, Lincoln's drafting and promulgation of the Emancipation Proclamation was a moment of conversion, which Pope Francis is always calling each Christian to in their own life. Even though Lincoln's conversion was not like the experience Day and Merton went through, it was a conversion with which we as human beings are very familiar. By invoking Lincoln, Francis offers a more nuanced idea of "greatness" that challenges the ethos of empire and structures of domination, and prizes openness to conversion. Even in the absence of Lincoln's personal conversion on slavery, he is "great" as an American leader because he shows his ability to set aside personal belief on slavery for what he considers to be a greater good for the people of the nation he has been elected to lead. It's not simple political expedience; it's a right judgment that comes first in his political life and might well have trickled down later in his personal beliefs as well. Moreover, the Church itself is familiar with this type of conversion.

This social conversion is a good explanation for what everyone goes through (or should go through) multiple times in the course of their lives. It is a conversion that need not entail making a drastic shift from one religion to a different one. Rather, it is a daily way of living one's life that requires being open to change and putting away that which closes us off to the world.[34] As with individuals, the Church must do the same thing. In this way, Lincoln's own conversion on emancipation as public policy is instructive for how the ecclesial con-version regarding slavery proceeded. If it was once accepted as part of the status quo, it would develop into a state of affairs that could never be tolerated or accepted under any circumstances.[35] Just as Lincoln went from being an individual who could accept slavery as conditional for the proper functioning of the Union, the Church went from a com-plete acceptance of slavery to a conditional acceptance of slavery, to an outright denunciation of the practice. In citing Lincoln, Francis also had a message for public figures, though its subtlety could be lost amid the popular impulse toward reification of Lincoln's image. And perhaps he could only have a small sense of what was to come.

Having said all of this, it would be unfair and uncritical not to point to one area of Lincoln's political statesmanship that was certainly not great. During the same apostolic pilgrimage during which Francis presided over the canonization of St. Junípero Serra, he also named Lincoln one of his great Americans. What were Indigenous peoples to have thought of either of these actions? For his part, Lincoln believed Native Americans were "inferior" and "wards of the Government."[36] This feeling manifested itself in the case of the Dakota 38. On Decem-ber 26, 1862, thirty-eight members of the Santee Sioux were executed after their involvement in a violent uprising earlier that year. W. Dale Mason enumerates other such events in Lincoln's presidency. One such occasion was "the Sand Creek Massacre in southeastern Colo-rado in November 1864. During an attack by the Third Colorado Regi-ment volunteers under Colonel John M. Chivington over four hundred Cheyenne and Arapaho were murdered. There is no recorded reaction by President Lincoln to the massacre."[37] Suffice it to say that Lincoln is not considered a liberator of Native Americans.

A Political Vocation:
The Public Role of Catholics Today

Part of the appeal of the Emancipation Proclamation to Lincoln was undoubtedly political. And what about Pope Francis and politics? It would be a grave mistake to believe that any ecclesiastical figure plays above the political realm, or that theology was apolitical. By its very nature, theology and the Church must be political in their interactions with the world. It is often remarked that the two issues that are unwelcome at any polite gathering are religion and politics. Even if that is true—and that my colleagues and I are frequently considered impolite company at these gatherings—it is also true that most Americans have a somewhat reductionist view of the word *politics*. We see especially in many of the liberation theologies of Latin America a particularly holistic understanding of political theology. For St. Óscar Romero, for instance, "politics, by definition, is anything that is connected to the life of the *polis* (the Greek word meaning 'city')."[38] The reduction, therefore, comes when folks believe that *political* means the same thing as *partisan*. Part of political life means participation in the public life of the world, which must tend especially to the needs of the poor.[39] Every Christian, then, is involved in political action because every individual is part of the city. But, in a unique way, there are certain women and men who take on positions of political leadership. In so doing, they are signing on to be responsible for the common good. Pope Francis has an idea for what that type of leadership must entail.

In his 2020 social encyclical *Fratelli Tutti*, Francis calls for "a better kind of politics" (nos. 154–97).[40] Within this document, Francis writes that we must strive toward a "political love." This is the first time in the corpus of Catholic social teaching that such a term has been used. Since Lincoln was the only professional politician that Francis mentioned during his address, it stands to reason that Lincoln's own political career is what Francis might have in mind for us when he endorses this type of political love. But what does this love entail? How did Lincoln embody it? How can public figures in our own day, especially with Catholics occupying some of the highest offices in the land, practice political love? First, Francis recognizes that to love another is not a one-time activity; rather, it represents a commitment over a long time. Therefore, Francis cites his prior writings on the topic from *Laudato Si'*: "What is needed is a politics which is far-sighted and capable of a new, integral, and interdisciplinary approach to handling the different aspects of the crisis" (*Fratelli Tutti* 177, citing *Laudato Si'* 197).[41] In this sense, Francis is showing his Ignatian colors. As a Jesuit, Francis is intimately familiar with St. Ignatius Loyola's writings on love.

In his *Spiritual Exercises*, Ignatius makes two points in his Contemplation to Attain the Love of God.[42] The first of these points is quite familiar: "Love ought to manifest itself in deeds rather than in words" (230). Or as St. Gregory the Great put it, "The proof of love is the performance of deeds." The second is less well-known: "Love consists in a mutual sharing of goods" (231). Since the *Spiritual Exercises* is meant as a how-to manual even for the exercitant, it could also be considered a book for political life. The entire manual seeks a congruence between two freedoms: human effort and divine grace. Even though Ignatius's expectation would have been that the retreatant would have completed the *Spiritual Exercises* by the time she arrived at the Contemplation to Attain the Love of God, this exercise is beneficial even without the others if the individual can recall that it is meant to be affective and entails a particular knowledge through experience of everything God has done for her. Moved with gratitude, she then returns it to God by carrying out good deeds, in love. This is fulfilled by the beautiful words of the Suscipe: "Take, Lord, and receive....You have given all this to me. I now return it to you" (234). Even though this contemplation was originally meant to be considered individually and in an interpersonal loving relationship, I argue that it is also appropriate for what Francis calls political love, and therefore can be extended to a real concern for the common good.

If love expresses itself in deeds rather than words, then talk is cheap! Moreover, authentic love means sharing what you have with the beloved. Anyone who has ever loved another and not felt love in return knows that unrequited love involves all giving and no receiving. For the political leader, love must take the same form. As Francis writes, "Political charity is born of a social awareness that transcends every individualistic mindset" (*Fratelli Tutti* 182). Just as true love between two individuals can never be about preserving oneself, true political love ought to be directed outward so that the commonweal is not only preserved but thrives. As Francis teaches, "When the good of others is at stake, good intentions are not enough. Concrete efforts must be made to bring about whatever they and their nations need for the sake of their development" (no. 185). Taking this very Ignatian definition of political love into consideration, it becomes clear why Francis chose Lincoln to highlight in his address. Lincoln's version of political love, which he discerned over a long time, was not fulfilled only by words or theory. Rather, Lincoln's love manifested more in deeds than in words. Even though the Emancipation Proclamation was written words, its effect was undeniable.

In considering political love, it is always necessary to consider what is realistically possible for the political leader. I say this not with a foreboding sense of doom that will require individuals to invoke violence in the name of realism.[43] In Lincoln's case, he knew that it was also his responsibility to save the Union. Even though Francis has often been critiqued as a utopian, he believes that political realism also can help the politician practice this special brand of love. In ensuring that all human beings enjoy fundamental human rights, Francis explains, "politicians are doers, builders with ambitious goals, possessed of a broad, realistic and pragmatic gaze that looks beyond their own borders" (*Fratelli Tutti* 188). What strikes Francis as realism strikes many observers as naïveté. And yet, Lincoln was able to do it. Francis makes explicit precisely what the architectural goal of politicians ought to be: "It is an act of charity to assist someone suffering, but it is also an act of charity, even if we do not know that person, to work to change the social conditions that caused his or her suffering. If someone helps an elderly person cross a river, that is a fine act of charity. The politician, on the other hand, builds a bridge, and that too is an act of charity" (no. 186).[44] Political love, like interpersonal love, entails taking risks. Most obviously, the politician who practices such charity can be in jeopardy of being physically harmed, if not murdered. Lincoln himself met this very fate at the hands of John Wilkes Booth, whose own racism led him to carry out the plot to assassinate Lincoln.[45] Even if Lincoln was not an antiracist by today's standard, he was most certainly killed because Booth believed him to be just that, and therefore posed a threat to the racist attitudes that Booth held in high esteem. Lincoln's legacy in the United States now is that of the preeminent bridge builder of all those who have ever worked in the Oval Office.

It is beyond debate that Lincoln is among the most revered Americans ever to have lived. Moreover, it can safely be said that when Francis identified him as one of his great Americans, most listeners nodded their heads in ready agreement. Francis encouraged the politicians listening to his address to follow in Lincoln's footsteps by building bridges in their own day and doing so by looking beyond their own personal needs toward the needs of all, especially the least, "in a spirit of openness to everyone" (*Fratelli Tutti* 190). Sitting behind the pope that day was then Vice President Joseph Biden, who in less than six years would become a successor to Lincoln as president of the United States and only the second Catholic ever to hold that office. His ascension to that post was not without controversy, especially among the United States

Catholic Bishops. This relationship is part of the story of what should be expected of political leaders, especially Catholic politicians, today.

What can Lincoln teach Catholic politicians about how they should embrace their leadership positions today? I suggest one surprising quality of Lincoln's tenure as president that can serve Biden and other Catholic politicians well: tenderness.[46] In the first place, Francis writes that tenderness "is love that draws near and becomes real. A movement that starts from our heart and reaches the eyes, the ears and the hands" (*Fratelli Tutti* 194). One of the most tender moments in Lincoln's career is the story of his interaction with Frederick Douglass at a public reception at the White House following Lincoln's second inaugural address on March 4, 1865. The evening before, Douglass had helped Kate Chase vest her father, Chief Justice Salmon Chase, in the robe he would wear to administer the oath of office to Lincoln for his second term. On the next day, after initially being denied entry on account of being Black, Douglass was ultimately admitted to the reception on Lincoln's explicit direction. Lincoln's tender love for Douglass was on full display, as Lincoln exclaimed, "Here comes my friend Douglass." As Douglass himself recounted, Lincoln took his friend by the hand and stated, "I am glad to see you. I saw you in the crowd to-day, listening to my inaugural address; how did you like it?"[47] The exchange between two friends, one of them a white man who was recently inaugurated for his second term as president of the United States, and the other a Black man who only moments earlier had been denied access to the affair due to his skin color, was momentous at this time and place.

I do not recount this story to make a savior out of Lincoln, nor do I contend that he was in a position of superiority over Douglass. Rather, what this story illustrates for us is what Ignatius, Pope Francis, and (I suspect) Lincoln and Douglass themselves would call mutual friendship. Lincoln literally extended his hand to Douglass in friendship on that day. The story does not end there, however. Douglass's response to Lincoln's query is historically, politically, and theologically significant: "Mr. Lincoln...that was a sacred effort."[48] In using the word *sacred* to describe the speech, Douglass speaks to the heart of Lincoln's second inaugural address, which is one of his most theological texts. He uttered these words concerning the two opposing forces whose bloody Civil War was only then coming to a long-awaited end, words that will forever be left to posterity:

Both read the same Bible, and pray to the same God; and each invokes His aid against the other. It may seem strange that any men should dare to ask a just God's assistance in wringing their bread from the sweat of other men's faces; but let us judge not that we be not judged. The prayers of both could not be answered; that of neither has been answered fully. The Almighty has His own purposes.[49]

One of the ancient names for "pope" since at least the end of the fifth century has been *pontifex*, which means "bridge builder."[50] Pope Francis, as I have shown above, has indicated that building bridges is essential in carrying out political love. One could scarcely imagine a moment more fraught with infighting than the time at which Lincoln delivered his second inaugural address. In spite of this, he sought to build a bridge. It is one over which we are still traversing today, even if there are moments when it appears that it will collapse. And so, it is of utmost importance to discern how to build a bridge in another moment of partisan divide.

When Joe Biden was elected the forty-sixth president of the United States, it happened despite the sharp dissent of many of the United States Catholic bishops.[51] This dissent found its origin in the revision of the document *Forming Consciences for Faithful Citizenship*,[52] which the United States Conference of Catholic Bishops (USCCB) revisits every four years in preparation for the presidential election and publishes as a way to provide background for Catholics who are discerning for whom to vote in the coming election. In the debate surrounding the revisions to the document at the November 2019 meeting of the USCCB, a rather remarkable exchange took place on the floor of the convention. It addressed the question of whether or not abortion represents the preeminent priority of the conference. At the center of the discussion were the words of Bishop Robert McElroy of San Diego:

> It is not Catholic teaching that abortion is the preeminent issue that we face in the world of Catholic social teaching. It is not. For us to say that, particularly when we omit the pope's articulation of this question…is a grave disservice to our people if we are trying to communicate to them what the magisterium teaches.

Archbishop Charles Chaput, then archbishop of Philadelphia, immediately rose to the floor to say that McElroy was guilty of setting up "an artificial battle between the bishops' conference of the United States and the Holy Father, which isn't true."

Why reference this debate in a discussion about what is expected of Catholics in public life today? Because it ought to be a central part of this type of vocation to have some relationship with the bishops of the country. This may seem like a quaint notion today, long after the days when Catholic prelates enjoyed a lofty stature in the minds of lay Catholics, and two decades after their credibility was shattered by their inept handling of the sexual abuse crisis that rocked the Church in the United States. Nevertheless, the bishops still function as important figures in the Church, and ought to be respected as teachers of the faith, especially by Catholic leaders in the political order. Second, this question is important to discuss because it is a two-way street: both bishops and politicians ought to look for ways to interact with due respect toward the other group. Both Lincoln and Francis can serve as models in this relationship.

First, Lincoln can model for Joe Biden and any other Catholic in political life how to engage in respectful dialogue with the bishops. When Lincoln promulgated the Emancipation Proclamation, there was yet a great deal that was unknown. He did not know if the document would be accepted, nor did he know what the ultimate outcome of the Civil War would be. And yet, as the Protestant theologian Reinhold Niebuhr concludes, "The only possibility of success for our nation and our culture in achieving the historic goals of peace and justice lies in our capacity to make sacrifices and to sustain endeavors without complete certainty of success."[53] Too often, American politicians, Catholic and non-Catholic, fall into the trap of believing that high ideals are impossible in public policy and in creating a more perfect union. This betrays an ultimate lack of belief that we can accomplish these lofty goals of justice and peace. Lincoln's example of searching for a way to save the union and end slavery remains the most daring and morally just decision an American president has ever made. Why can't this achievement be duplicated today? One answer to that question is that we do not have a moral cause that rises to the gravity of slavery plaguing our nation. The bishops of the United States would disagree with this contention; they propose that the legalization of abortion is just such a plague and sinks to the same level of moral decrepitude as chattel slavery. While Catholic elected officials are not responsible for governing based on the magisterial teachings of the Church, nor are they free to ignore these teachings. They would be well served to work for some fruitful dialogue, in good faith, with the bishops on areas where they disagree, especially abortion.

The question of abortion is more complex than either the bishops or the pro-choice politicians make it out to be.[54] While it is Catholic teaching that direct abortion may never be justified under any circumstance, the vast majority of Catholics would disagree with this teaching. As Charles Camosy notes, "This reality, of course, does not fit into our lazy and imprecise 'pro-life' vs. 'pro-choice' sound-bite rhetoric."[55] This rhetoric has hardly changed since *Roe v. Wade* was decided.[56] Here I propose that two Catholic moralists, Richard A. McCormick, SJ, and Julie Hanlon Rubio, provide helpful measures against this "lazy rhetoric" today in that they both advance a more nuanced position, and one that befits the legacy of Lincoln's bridge building. Sometimes a national-level policy is necessary to carry out justice; other times, it is not as effective. As Rubio argues, when it comes to authentic pro-life advocacy, "the most important work to be done lies at the local level—in particular, in efforts to empower young adults to see themselves and their relationships differently and in efforts to encourage caregiving in communities."[57]

How are Catholic politicians advancing this cause? Are grassroots-level activists working only with the goal of prohibiting abortion through overturning state laws in the wake of *Dobbs v. Jackson*? Or can liberals and conservatives work together to decrease the abortion rate through the means that Rubio suggests?[58] Too often we find the two major political parties in the United States at an impasse on the issue of abortion. Fair enough. But what then proceeds is mudslinging that one side wants to kill babies, while the other side is sexist and hates women. This type of reductive, deliberately inflammatory rhetoric is fruitless, and ought to be discontinued and derided especially by those in governmental leadership who appear daily in various news media. The answer is to search for a middle way on this issue.

Such a middle way is presented in McCormick's work. Although he came to this conclusion searching for a middle ground in 1989, his elements for such a position remain timely.[59] Even though McCormick was searching for a middle ground, not every individual will agree with all of his elements. One of McCormick's elements of a middle way is that "there should be alternatives to abortion."[60] Even people who believe that women should have the right to choose whether or not to carry a pregnancy to term should agree that abortion ought not be her only recourse in the case of an unintended pregnancy. Second, McCormick argues, "The causes that lead to abortion should be abolished insofar as possible."[61] A frequently used trope during campaign season is that when Democrats are in office, the number of abortions is reduced because of other economic policies that are carried out during these years. While that is a fair argument, it belies the rest of the liberal talking points that almost exclusively privilege the right to abortion over prenatal rights of the child in the womb. On the other hand, Republicans were so obsessed with the overturn of *Roe v. Wade* that any discussion of *reducing* abortions is disqualified out of hand. This is a ridiculous impasse. Both sides can make room here without actually compromising what is most important to them. Third, McCormick argues, "Whenever a discussion becomes heated, it should cease."[62] By reducing individuals to murderers or sexists, we debase the public forum. This is all the more apropos when Catholic bishops are to blame for the heat.

I return, then, to the aforementioned November 2019 bishops' debate about the emphasis on abortion as the preeminent issue in Church teaching today. McElroy's dissent from the final document, as published, is accurate. The burden of proof is on the bishops for showing that it has been *the* preeminent priority in magisterial pronouncements. In their document, they never do this. McElroy, for his part, has shown that abortion is *a* preeminent priority, but not *the* preeminent priority.[63] The difference between the definite and indefinite articles, in this case, is substantial. Unfortunately, the USCCB has decided on the definite article, and they have advanced a line of argumentation that is cultural warfare. The predictable outcome has been that many in the conference have advocated for Biden and other pro-choice Catholic politicians to be prohibited from receiving the Eucharist.[64] But this directly contravenes another of Pope Francis's statements during his 2015 apostolic pilgrimage to the United States. In his address to the Bishops of the United States at the Cathedral of St. Matthew in Washington, Francis called over and again for them to dialogue with others, and admonished them in no uncertain terms: "Harsh and divisive language does not befit the tongue of a pastor, it has no place in his heart; although it may momentarily seem to win the day, only the enduring allure of goodness and love remains truly convincing."[65] No words ever uttered by a pope have ever condemned cultural warfare in clearer terms. Less than twenty-four hours later, Francis would address a different group of American leaders: those in Congress. On that day, he invoked Lincoln, a beloved and revered political icon of American history and a man whose penchant for listening to and dialoguing with those who held different viewpoints is nearly unparalleled in American history. Lincoln was, for Pope Francis, and for us, a model of the type of dialogue that he wishes of Catholic politicians and bishops. In modeling this type of prophetic leadership, Lincoln paved the way for liberation and more pervasive human rights. It is fitting that nearly a century after his untimely death, a prophetic Black man delivered his most famous speech under the watchful gaze of Lincoln's towering memorial. It is to this great American, Martin Luther King Jr., that I now turn.

Chapter Two

MARTIN LUTHER KING JR. AND BLACK LIVES MATTER

Ours has been a religious home, and this too has made this burden easier to bear. Our concern now is that his work does not die. He gave his life for the poor of the world—the garbage workers of Memphis and the peasants of Vietnam. Nothing hurt him more than that man could attempt no way to solve problems except through violence. He gave his life in search of a more excellent way, a more effective way, a creative rather than destructive way.

—Coretta Scott King[1]

Martin Luther King Jr. was not Catholic. Nevertheless, fifty years to the day after his April 4, 1968, assassination, seven white Catholic activists utilized King's example of nonviolent direct action to trespass onto the Naval Submarine Base Kings Bay and deface property on the base, including but not limited to the nuclear weapons that have the potential to wreak havoc on the world's population. In their Action Statement, this group, known as the "Kings Bay Seven," cited only three sources: King, Pope Francis, and the prophecy in Isaiah 2 that says that in times to come, people of faith will "beat swords into plowshares."[2] These three citations, of course, reflect the will of the members of the Kings Bay Seven that we will one day see an end not only to the use of nuclear weapons on human beings and the entirety of God's creation, but also to the very manufacture of such devices. In this chapter, I examine what led these peace activists to carry out their action as a commemoration of King's life and death. Moreover, as with the other great Americans, I will place King into conversation with Pope Francis. Why did Francis choose King?

The first section of this chapter deals with the civil rights movement. While it is necessarily brief, it will serve to place King in context. Why was he important in the middle of the twentieth century, and why might he continue to be important today? What did the movement set out to accomplish? Did it succeed or was there work yet to be accomplished? What do most Americans learn about civil rights today and how might that curriculum be amended to account for the reality more accurately? This section of the chapter also examines the role the Catholic Church played during the civil rights movement. Today, Catholic social teaching still calls for civil rights along with concomitant civil responsibilities that all human beings share. This calling is all part of a larger picture that envisions a society in which all people will join with nonhuman creation in bringing about the universal common good.

In the second section of this chapter, I turn to the words and lifework of King himself. What made him tick? How was he formed in a Christian ideology that caused him to work for justice, and preach for justice? More importantly, how did King see the Church in the grander scheme of replying to the injustices that surround us in the world today? The Church possesses instruction from Jesus himself on its role in society. In particular, Jesus's commandment to love one another plays an outsized role in bringing to mind the Christian response to societal realities. How did King believe we ought to love God and love our neighbor as ourselves? In this section of the chapter, I dive more deeply into King's religious and philosophical formation as well as the gracious words he spoke, which likely caused Francis to take notice of this great American.

In the concluding section of the chapter, I consider King and antiracism to suggest that King is the ideal figure for building an antiracist American Church today. I argue that King and the civil rights movement are the precursors to the contemporary Black Lives Matter movement in the United States. This link has been denied by some,[3] but this denial is partly due to the same factors that led people to deny the righteousness of the civil rights activists in the previous century. Today, the Catholic Church in the United States is reluctant to embrace Black Lives Matter, but it must if the Church is to live up to its high call and the dignity of being children of God.[4] In the theological analysis of Bryan Massingale, the Church must take upon itself King's priority: to become "the beloved community."[5] The chapter ends with some concrete practices that might carry out this dream. But the dream itself began because there was a nightmare.[6] I will now discuss why King had to dream in the first place.

A Dream Yet to Be Fulfilled: Civil Rights Then and Now

Without any question, King is an eminent figure among many contemporaries in the civil rights movement in the United States.[7] In fact, he has become synonymous with the movement itself, even if he was surrounded by legendary figures on all sides during those fateful years. But when Pope Francis named King one of his great Americans in his address, he specifically mentioned the march that King led from Selma to Montgomery, Alabama. Andrew Young describes the event that was the genesis of the march: "On February 17 [1965], following a tension-charged night march in Marion, a group of marchers and members of the press were brutally attacked by the Marion police and Alabama state troopers. During the attack, Jimmy Lee Jackson, a black Vietnam veteran, was shot when he went to the aid of his mother, who was also in the march."[8] The environment in the United States at the time is well known through pictures, film, and documentary items that show how Black people were at the mercy of the authorities. So, when the marches had been completed, King's rhetoric showed what civil rights meant, particularly to him and those with whom he worked closely.

King's speech on March 25, 1965, marked the end of the five-day journey from Selma to Montgomery. But it also echoed the unrealized dream that he shared with his companions in the movement. King's understanding of civil rights meant something different than his other contemporaries, both religious and not. Why did Black people need to claim and assert their civil rights in the first place? For King, there are "triple evils." In an address on April 16, 1967, King spoke these words: "Now, when I say question the whole society, it means ultimately coming to see that the problem of racism, the problem of economic exploitation, and the problem of war are all tied together."[9] What is fascinating if not unsurprising, if we also consider Pope Francis's own message, as well as the lives of the other great Americans, is the very next paragraph of King's speech that day. King, ever the preacher, cites Jesus's interaction with Nicodemus from the Gospel of John: "Jesus looked at him and said, 'Nicodemus, you must be born again.'"[10] For King and his colleagues, the civil rights movement recognized the triple evils and sought a national conversion. As I highlight throughout this volume, we make a profound error when we limit conversion to religious language. Conversion involves complete renunciation of those things that have kept us from being fully human in the past and movement toward that which will make us more truly ourselves.

Pope Francis, in calling King a great American, was likely speaking on behalf of many in the chamber that day, as well as countless others who know King for the very "dream" that Francis cited in his address. Each January when King is commemorated, his most famous speech, which he delivered in front of the Lincoln Memorial on August 28, 1963, is replayed. During this keynote address of the March on Washington for civil rights, King began by citing Francis's other great American, Abraham Lincoln. But what led King to that moment? And who led him there? In his address, Francis immediately pivots to call attention to the dream of many immigrants and refugees who seek a better life for themselves and their families in the United States. As King's biographer, David Lewis, notes, the phrase "I have a dream" did not debut in the Washington speech with which we are all so familiar. King used those words a number of times during a speech in Detroit's Cobo Hall on June 23, 1963.[11] Even if Lewis contends that the March has become the subject of "mythomania," it is obvious that Pope Francis did not fall victim to such an interpretation.[12]

Pope Francis praises King for his dream and notes that this theme of King's speeches at the time was also a theme of the United States as a whole. If the "American Dream" is truly for every inhabitant of the United States, then it must result in civil rights for all, especially those who had been denied. This section of Francis's address is perhaps his most prophetic; this is fitting since in King he was talking about a great prophet. As I noted above, one of the triple evils of the United States, according to King, was economic exploitation. Therefore, King's dream is more expansive than racial justice alone, even if the most famous line has to do with exactly that. The March on Washington was multivalent in its goals, which did not please everyone who had initially wanted to participate:

> The introduction of Kennedy's civil rights bill altered activists' agendas, as the coalition widened to include mainstream civil rights groups, white churches, and progressive labor unions. Many who dreamed of militant civil disobedience or a dramatic demonstration of the economic crisis of black America saw only fatal compromises of the march's methods and goals.[13]

The context in which King anchored the civil rights movement, however, is complex. The complexity is due not to a disagreement over the fundamental issue at stake, which was the liberation of Black people in the United States. This movement's goal was that all human beings would share the human rights granted to all by their Creator at birth. The complexity came with the fundamental disagreement concerning *how* to reach this goal. One approach that was very popular among activists in the 1950s and 1960s held that violence was the only means to the end for which they longed. King's view was the polar opposite. One of the most prominent Black theologians of the twentieth century, James H. Cone, put the dilemma like this: "For me, the burning theological question was, how can I reconcile Christianity and Black Power, Martin Luther King's idea of nonviolence and Malcolm X's 'by any means necessary' philosophy?"[14] In fact, as Taylor Branch argues at the very end of his trilogy on King's America,

> King himself upheld nonviolence until he was nearly alone among colleagues weary of sacrifice. To the end, he resisted incitements to violence, cynicism, and tribal retreat. He grasped freedom seen and unseen, rooted in ecumenical faith, sustaining patriotism to brighten the heritage of his country for all people. These treasures abide with lasting promise from America in the King years.[15]

However, to study King is also to be convinced that he himself received a great many treasures, including the pearl of great price (see Matt 13:46). How did that impact his life and mission? One answer lies in how he shared these treasures with others.

King and Neighbor Love: Rereading the Gospel Command to Love

The central way to interpret King's activism in the civil rights movement is to view it in light of his leadership in the Christian community as a pastor. Later in this volume, I will address Dorothy Day's personalism. King, likewise, was influenced by a Christian personalism that accounted for much of his discourse in the ecclesial and public realm.[16] This Christian personalism led King to a position whereby he preached *agape*. This notion of love, which is foundational in the New Testament, was also foundational in King's ideology. But it was not universally appreciated by Black theologians. As Cone puts the issue, King's insistence on love meant that it was important for Black people to love the white people who systematically and literally put them to death. Or, as Cone concludes, "One cannot help but think that most whites 'loved' Martin Luther King, Jr., not because of his attempt to free his people, but because his approach was the least threatening to the white power structure."[17] To be sure, there is an issue there, and a sincere question that takes us back to the very reason for Cone's study in the first place: Whose approach to the civil rights question was better suited to solving the problems at hand, King's or Malcolm X's? Here, I would contend that both figures clearly had the well-being of Black Americans in mind; yet there is a reason that Pope Francis chose to point to King in his "great Americans" address. A likely explanation for Francis's choice is King's insistence on neighbor love.

King's own philosophy of love was intimately connected with his directive of absolute dedication to gospel nonviolence. The two were inseparable in his worldview. As he wrote in 1958, there are six unique characteristics of the nonviolent resistance in which he and his coworkers engaged: it is not cowardly; it is not about humiliating the opponent; it is directed against evil itself, rather than persons who are doing evil things; it is willing to accept suffering rather than delivering it to others; it avoids not only external, but also interior violence; and finally, "it is based on the conviction that the universe in on the side of justice."[18] The fifth characteristic listed provides King an opportunity to reflect on the meaning of love in the movement of nonviolent resistance: "The nonviolent resister not only refuses to shoot his opponent but he also refuses to hate him. At the center of nonviolence stands the principle of love."[19] Herein lies the major critique that Cone and others had of King's philosophy of nonviolence and love. As Vincent Harding writes, "The white man no longer exists. He is not to be lived with and he is not to be destroyed. He is simply to be ignored."[20] This approach differs from King's dream for civil rights, which I have elaborated above. Even if Cone disagreed with King's approach, he saw a lasting impact that was essential for Black Christianity:

> To be sure, one may argue that his method of nonviolence did not meet the needs of the black community in an age of black power; but it is beyond question that it was King's influence and leadership in the black community which brought us to the period in which we now live, and for that we are in debt.[21]

Despite Malcolm X's or Cone's or others' misgivings, King pressed on because he believed the nonviolence that sprung from love was a higher calling, one befitting the Christian. In a particular way, King examines the three Greek words for love: *eros*, *philia*, and *agape*. Noting that the first two mean romantic love and love between friends, respectively, King draws attention instead to the virtuous *agapic* love that comes from God.[22] The latter type of love, King notes, is "disinterested love. It is a love in which the individual seeks not his own good, but the good of his neighbor (1 Cor 10:24). *Agape* does not begin by discriminating between worthy and unworthy people, or any qualities people possess. It begins by loving others *for their sakes*."[23] Many human beings have experienced precisely this kind of love from their parents, grandparents, other family members, or close friends. That is to say, for instance, one's spouse will often be the source and object of the love of *eros*; however, if that is the only type of love present, the relationship will be in serious danger. Authentic marital love ought to transcend erotic love and be a love that is "an overflowing love that seeks nothing in return."[24] Likewise, if one is fortunate enough to have friends

39

who are close to them in ways that mean they give of their time and resources to be an intimate part of their friends' lives, then their love is no longer only *philia*. It has moved to *agapic* love, which is embodied most perfectly by Christ, in that it is "directed to the beloved for the beloved's sake."[25] Throughout the COVID pandemic that ravaged the world, one of the most moving features of the evening news broadcasts in the United States was the video footage from rooftops, balconies, and windows of apartment buildings in New York City, where the residents would cheer their gratitude for first responders and healthcare workers during the shift change at the city's hospitals. Those workers, even though they were doing their jobs, went above and beyond, at risk of their safety and the safety of their families for their patients' sakes. Their *agapic* service to their patients, and the daily, public expressions of thanks from the community, were extraordinarily moving to witness.

Agape, as King makes clear, actually has nothing to do with liking another person. This is the major way in which King parts company with Malcolm X, Harding, and Cone. King reflects,

> Liking is an affectionate emotion, and I can't like anybody who would bomb my home. I can't like anybody who would exploit me. I can't like anybody who would trample over me with injustices. I can't like them. I can't like anybody who threatens to kill me day in and day out. But Jesus reminds us that love is greater than liking.[26]

Both King and Pope Francis are among the Christian figures who point to the story of the Good Samaritan in explaining what *agape* is and what it requires of the individual looking to make that story her own. As King writes, "The Samaritan who helped the Jew on the Jericho Road was 'good' because he responded to the human need that he was presented with."[27] When Francis cites the Golden Rule during his analysis of King's greatness in his address, he explicitly raises a major problem in the United States: the temptation "to discard whatever proves troublesome." The story of the Good Samaritan, as Francis notes at some length, is the quintessential example of the throwaway culture that he decries over and again.[28]

The clearest overlap between King and Francis, though, is that neither is content with doing a simple exegesis of the Good Samaritan story as it appears in Luke 10:25–37. Both find common ground in turning the story into a provocation for reflection on our own lives. As Francis pointedly asks, "Which of these characters do you resemble?" (*Fratelli Tutti* 64). While this is an essential question for each individual to answer with her own actions on a daily basis, Francis notes that there are no limits to how we show our love in our lives. Nothing can stand in the way of our becoming neighbors to all other people in the world, but we must embody that through the way we care for the weakest among us. The example that Jesus offers in this pericope must take pride of place, writes Francis in *Fratelli Tutti*: "This encounter of mercy between a Samaritan and a Jew is highly provocative; it leaves no room for ideological manipulation and challenges us to expand our frontiers. It gives a universal dimension to our call to love, one that transcends all prejudices, all historical barriers, all petty interests" (no. 83). Reading such a reflection makes it obvious why Francis would select King as one of his great Americans. King's approach to the question of love was that it must overcome every animus that we hold, even to the point of loving those whom we do not like. For each person, *agape* means discerning what is going on in life right now and then deciding what needs to be done in order to love most concretely in action, in deeds, and not just words, as I noted in chapter 1.

King's understanding of *agape* in his own life, and in American society at the time, was dominated by the racial injustice that was being carried out on a large scale and enforced by the police. King explains the reality of putting the story of the Good Samaritan into practice for him in the 1960s: "Since the white man's personality is greatly distorted by segregation, and his soul is greatly scarred, he needs the love of the Negro. The Negro must love the white man, because the white man needs his love to remove his tensions, insecurities, and fears."[29] These words show precisely the intellectual impact of Gandhi on King's own writing and activism. As King states in explicating his own theory of nonviolent resistance, "We shall match your capacity to inflict suffering by our capacity to endure suffering. We will meet your physical force with soul force. Do to us what you will and we will still love you."[30] Both King and Gandhi (even though he wasn't a Christian) took their ethical cues from Jesus's example of nonviolence in scripture. As King remarks in his autobiography, "Gandhi was probably the first person in history to lift the love ethic of Jesus above mere interaction between individuals to a powerful and effective social force on a large scale."[31] Rather than falling victim to the common trope that

41

pacifism is passive (because of the similarity in etymology), King notes that "*agape* is not a weak, passive love." He continues by calling to mind precisely the teachings of Jesus from the Gospels that stand out in *agapic* love in the world today:

> It doesn't stop at the first mile, but it goes the second mile to restore community. It is a willingness to forgive, not seven times, but seventy times seven to restore community. The cross is the eternal expression of the length to which God will go in order to restore broken community. The resurrection is a symbol of God's triumph over all the forces that seek to block community.[32]

Quite simply, King was driven by his attention to the gospel; it is no wonder that Pope Francis saw in King's own discourse and, even more, in his actions of nonviolent resistance, a kindred spirit that would be able to lead America forward.

Another part of King's life that undoubtedly stood out for Francis is the way King refused to compartmentalize different facets of life and injustices that plagued society. I have already shown above how King believed that there were "triple evils" in the United States that couldn't be separated from each other. This sense of an integral whole also was at the heart of King's understanding of *agape* love, which led to nonviolence. Moreover, in his discussion on *agape*, King utilizes terminology that would later be so closely tied in with Francis's magisterium that the very same words could summarize the social encyclical *Laudato Si'*: "In the final analysis, *agape* means a recognition of the fact that all life is interrelated."[33] In *Laudato Si'*, Francis reflects on many scriptural accounts, and concludes, "These ancient stories, full of symbolism, bear witness to a conviction which we today share, that everything is interconnected, and that genuine care for our own lives and our relationships with nature is inseparable from fraternity, justice and faithfulness to others" (no. 70). As I will note later in my discussion of Dorothy Day, King's insistence that we are complex creatures who are connected with all other people on the planet was essential in his coming to the conclusion that violent resistance was never an adequate response to the evils he and other Black Americans faced in the United States. Likewise, Francis takes this concept even a step further by noting that we are not only interrelated to our human

brothers and sisters, but even to nonhuman creation. King is a forerun-
ner to such a religious worldview. How would King respond today? He
would advocate for antiracism.

Becoming an Antiracist Church: Black Lives Matter and Catholic Social Teaching

How did King get to the point in his thinking where he was
directed by the Gospels? He came to this point in his public ministry because he was convinced that Jesus's ministry ought to guide his
own as a Christian pastor in the twentieth century. That is the same
conviction Christian pastors have had throughout the centuries. They
have followed a tried and true threefold practice: see, judge, and act,
first named as such by Cardinal Joseph Cardijn, but enacted for two
millennia and counting.[34] Therefore, Christians must enact the same
measures of being faithful to the gospel as they have always done. In
order to seek out justice for the poor and oppressed today, Christians
must motivate themselves with the same command that has always
motivated them: "Do unto others as you would have them do unto
you." When Francis uttered those words during his 2015 address, as he
recalled the valiant life and times of King, he was also urging onward
all those in the room with him—many of them legislators with great
power to enact justice through the passage and reform of law—and
indeed, everyone watching or listening to him deliver the address. He
was reminding us of Christ's own instruction, which is meant to be the
core of the daily Christian practice.

There is a constant need for people to fight for the civil rights of
various groups who are the objects of injustice in our society. I refer in
these pages to many of these groups, but we all know the people in our
own communities who are most in need of solidarity. Pope Francis has
reminded us that we cannot leave it to others to care for those in the
greatest need. As he rightly notes in his analysis of the story of the Good
Samaritan, those who ignored the victim on the road were the religious
professionals of their day (*Fratelli Tutti* 74). We are all too familiar with
the pitfalls of trusting clergy and religious leaders of our own day to
be perfect, to have and model all the right answers to societal ills, or
to be on the front lines in times of great injustice. Particularly in the

43

Catholic Church, this moral chasm seems all the more evident. I need not elaborate at great length in any one of these areas, but only in our recent memory, the Catholic Church in the United States has been rocked by various levels of a sexual abuse scandal wherein ordained priests sexually molested and otherwise abused minors, with their bishops and religious superiors keeping that information secret; those same bishops and their successors have largely allied themselves with the GOP in the United States on the sole basis of one issue, abortion, which they deem to be of preeminent moral gravity; when tragedies occur, precious few bishops or Catholic clergy come to the forefront as King had done (with Catholic clergy in tow) only sixty years earlier.[35] These failings have reached a crescendo in the bishops' collective silence on the Black Lives Matter movement that has swept across the United States in the last years.

When students and faculty returned to campus in the midst of the COVID-19 pandemic to begin the 2020–21 academic year at my former community, Marywood University in Scranton, Pennsylvania, we did not know what to expect. We knew that many classes would be held in a hybrid format, meeting both in person and online; that was new for us all, to say the least. We knew that when we were on campus, we had to wear masks; a necessary discomfort, to be sure. But we were caught off-guard by the large sign that graced the space directly in eyeshot upon entering the campus: BLACK LIVES MATTER. The president of the university, Sister Mary Persico, IHM, received criticism and even backlash from the local community.[36] Our university, of course, was not the only academic or religiously sponsored community to express solidarity with the movement itself. Yet the U.S. Catholic Church's support for the movement has been anemic. Pope Francis has been very clear on the issue. In a book-length discussion with journalist Austen Ivereigh, Francis decried narcissism:

> You'll never find such people protesting the death of George Floyd, or joining a demonstration because there are shantytowns where children lack water or education, or because there are whole families who have lost their income. You won't find them protesting the astonishing amounts spent on the arms trade [that] could be used to feed the whole of the human race and school every child. On such matters

44

they would never protest; they are incapable of moving outside of their own little world of interests.[37]

Like King, Francis sees how the injustices of society are linked to one another. In this brief passage, Francis alludes to King's triple evils of racism, militarism, and poverty. There is always a danger in assuming we would know what a historical figure would do if he or she were alive today. However, in this instance, it is almost a certainty that King would be a central figure in the Black Lives Matter movement. Why isn't the Catholic Church?[38]

Black Lives Matter has been sustained on many levels by the presence and organization of many religious leaders. But as Olga Segura has pointedly asked, "How can the U.S. Bishops show Black people that they are genuinely listening and committed to the struggle for liberation?"[39] Anyone who has ever been involved in almost any line of work or ministry knows the importance of listening to others before arriving at an important decision. Pope Francis has often reflected on the importance of listening in his own teachings. It seems that if the bishops are ever going to get to the point of answering this question adequately, they must first listen to their people, especially Black people, in their congregations and beyond, seeking insights from those who do not identify as Catholic. Only when the bishops do this will they even approach a response that is not tone-deaf or patronizing. Thus far, the bishops have been very weak on this issue. To date, the most significant way the U.S. bishops have responded to Black Lives Matter is through their 2018 pastoral letter, "Open Wide Our Hearts: The Enduring Call to Love."[40] This follows in a succession of pastoral letters on racism throughout the episcopal conference's history.[41] Even these documents, however, were written within a context of an episcopal conference that has a terrible history when it comes to dealing with racism in the United States.[42] In their 2018 installment, the bishops do make a number of helpful propositions that advance the cause of racial justice in the United States. Most poignantly, they underscore the importance of "changing structures" and the necessity of the "conversion of all."[43] As they discuss structural change, the bishops cite both King and Francis's 2015 Address. This is a step forward because it recognizes that the sin and injustice that we are experiencing is more than what Massingale refers to as "common sense racism."[44] The letter needed to accomplish more.

The bishops' letter was insufficient, partially because it did not define its terms rigorously (or even accurately) and refused to grapple with the messy reality of racial injustice in the United States. The result was all too predictable: "Some of the...failures of the pastoral document include an incorrect definition of racism, no mention of white supremacy, and no acknowledgment of the Black Lives Matter movement....They apologized for the church's failings to live Christ-like but made no mention of what these times are or the church's participation in chattel slavery."[45] This is not only obviously insufficient, but it has even more dire ramifications. Because American Catholicism has been so integrally connected with racism in the United States, the only way out of this relationship is explicit condemnation of racism coupled with actual antiracist behavior.[46] The bishops are correct, however, in pointing to one potential solution to the crisis before us. They explicitly endorse King's penchant for bringing together various Christian bodies and people of all faiths (and none) in working together for a common goal. They conclude, "That spirit is integral to the fight today, and in some communities, the success of this effort will very much depend on this kind of collaboration."[47]

I have already addressed King's religious motivation for doing what he did. But that religious worldview extended to a natural coexistence with other clergy and religious leaders of various stripes. The most obvious partnership between King and the Catholic hierarchy took place on September 18, 1964. On that occasion, "the pope endorsed America's nonviolent civil rights movement, and promised he would issue a statement condemning racial segregation and discrimination."[48] That whole meeting could have been scrapped if the efforts of Cardinal Francis Spellman had come to fruition. Spellman worked at the behest of J. Edgar Hoover to cancel the audience before it could ever take place.[49] In an early paper, written while he was a student at Crozer Theological Seminary, King wrote a remarkable analysis of the French Catholic philosopher Jacques Maritain.[50] It is so remarkable because King's conclusion is a line of thinking that he would extend throughout his ministry and public activism, vis-à-vis Catholicism: "For [Maritain], Catholics are not Catholicism, and the errors, apathies, shortcomings and slumbers of Catholics do not involve Catholicism."[51] This is instructive because it is a helpful reminder that no religious community ought to be defined by the worst actions of a given practitioner, or even of the bishops. King was, quite simply, open to working with any figure (religious or not) who believed in the same principles for which he gave his life. This is part of the reason Pope Francis holds him in such high esteem. But how ought King influence the Church today?

King's own theology is paradigmatic of how the Catholic Church can and should embrace Black Lives Matter in its ecclesiology today. Segura lists a number of concrete steps the Church should take right away to ally itself with the Black Lives Matter movement. She argues that the Church must begin by "first, creating a website for the Ad Hoc Committee Against Racism (ACAR) so that Catholics can see the ongoing work of the USCCB's antiracism group....Second, Pope Francis should call for and attend a gathering in the United States to encourage bishops to address the issue of race....Third, dioceses across the country must develop antiracism training for all clergy in formation."[52] I wholeheartedly agree with all of these steps, although I would add that the USCCB should drop the "ad hoc" designation and vote to make the Committee Against Racism a permanent part of the conference's structure, lest we think that the problem will be solved overnight; they could also change "racism" to "white supremacy" in the name of the committee. But how can the Church in the United States accomplish these goals? We would do well to learn from King's own teachings on the matter, in addition to the way in which he walked with all those interested in working for peace and justice. I propose as a Kingian model for the Church four "programs and prospects" near and dear to his own heart.[53]

The first of these steps is education. As King laments, "The sad truth is that American schools, by and large, do not know how to teach—nor frequently what to teach."[54] All the more can we say this about Catholic schools in the United States, both those sponsored by dioceses and those sponsored by religious orders. This is true from prekindergarten level even to graduate education. Bishops, religious superiors, directors of faith formation, and lay administrators in the Church need to make antiracism part of each semester's curriculum. This obviously means that Black History Month can no longer be an outlier in the school year. Rather, students should be taught at all grade levels in Church-sponsored institutions about the racism that is inherent in the United States. Then, once they've learned about the past and the present in our country, their Catholic education will only be as valuable as the impetus it gives its students to do something in their communities that is antiracist. Segura notes one of the most important levels of education where this is necessary: the seminary. If priests would preach more about the white privilege and racism that continues to surround us, every Catholic in the pews would be educated on a weekly basis. This trickles down into the home. The sooner that American Catholics see the connection between their faith and antiracism, the sooner there will be a change in the domestic Church. Bryan Massingale reminds us that the Church already has the tools to carry out such a change in education: conversion, baptism, and Eucharist.[55]

The second program King suggests is employment. King especially points to "human services." He notes that these jobs, "medical attention, social services, neighborhood amenities of various kinds— are in scarce supply in this country, especially in localities of poverty…. The traditional job requirements are a barrier to attaining an adequate supply of personnel, especially if the number of jobs expands to meet the existing need."[56] King's critique here is twofold. First, he recognizes that the capitalist system in the United States is structured in such a way that the poor are never able to "pull themselves up by their bootstraps." King moved toward democratic socialism[57] as an alternative to the poverty overwhelming Black communities in the United States during the 1950s and '60s. The same response has gained popular support today, especially among followers of Senator Bernie Sanders. The Church ought to take on this same approach in order to work for the poor, many of whom are people of color and whose poverty is linked to race by deeply rooted systemic injustice in this country. Since Catholic social teaching has long been on the side of the worker and has fought for an end to poverty, it would only seem natural that this would be a place where the Church could have a profound impact. Chancery offices, pastoral centers, schools, and universities ought to employ people who may not meet "the traditional job requirements." The Church ought to be a place where every worker thrives with a living wage. Second, King points his finger at higher education.[58] Catholic colleges and universities must become creative, offering new opportunities to people who may have never dreamed of going to college. There should be more places like Arrupe College, the two-year institution affiliated with Loyola University, Chicago.[59] The link between education and employment is most fruitfully made, however, in the Cristo Rey network of schools that have reenvisioned how these two components of life are connected.[60] King would want more of these schools.

The third area that King highlighted was "rights." Nearly sixty years ago, King lamented the reality for Black Americans: "The new forms of rights are new methods of participation in decision-making. The concept of democracy is being pushed to deeper levels of meaning—from formal exercise of voting, still an issue in much of the United States for many Negroes, to effective participation in major decisions."[61] Rights and participation are foundational principles of Catholic social teaching, so this is another program that should be easy for the Church to support. And yet, where was the voice of the USCCB when voting rights laws were being restricted in various states in early 2021? They were almost entirely silent.[62] Bishops should be protesting such legislative decisions as loudly as they protest abortion. If the bishops are serious about being antiracist in the twenty-first century, they must be abundantly clear that voting rights must never be taken away from people of color. The Black Lives Matter movement is proposing an agenda that fights for those who have been constantly seen as outsiders and, in many cases, as unworthy of any human dignity whatsoever. This should sound a clarion call in the bishops' conference to work for justice for those marginalized groups. To do so, they do not have to propose any novelty in Catholic social thought, but only must work with the very foundations of this system.

Fourth, and finally, King pointed to housing. King prophetically exclaims,

> New, good housing available at low cost is needed to satisfy the dwelling needs of the underclass....Once more priorities have to be reversed; the federal government subsidizes the nonpoor twice as much as the poor when we include various forms of subsidies such as middle-income public housing, tax deductions for mortgage interest and real estate taxes.[63]

As I will discuss in the next chapter on Dorothy Day, all of the recent popes have been consistent in proclaiming that we need a reevaluation of priorities when it comes to work: labor is for the human, not vice versa. In this case, King makes a similar point about housing. He decries the ghettos that exist in the United States as permanent places of residence. While he believes they are adequate for temporary housing, he is also clearsighted about their limits. Why is the Church not leading the way with funding affordable housing for the poor? Why hasn't the Church spoken against redlining? As soon as preachers and teachers in the Church begin speaking publicly about white privilege, it will be clear to many parishioners that even if they have worked hard for their resources, their status in life is also likely a benefit of being born white. As Massingale puts it, white privilege is "the uneven and unfair distribution of power, privilege, land, and material resources favoring white people. White privilege is not an abstraction; it is real."[64] As soon as the Church reckons with the reality of white privilege, the entire community can begin seeing the ways in which the Body of Christ has been scarred by racism in its midst. Only when bishops and those in leadership positions make antiracism a priority will it be possible for the Church to commit to Black Lives Matter with passion.[65] As Pope Francis asked of us above, which of the characters in the story of the Good Samaritan does the Church resemble?

Pope Francis entitled his 2020 book *Let Us Dream*. It is no secret that King's most famous words were "I have a dream." King is, perhaps, the most obvious choice that Francis had for a "great American." King embodied the type of dreaming in which Francis wants all of us to engage. To dream for a better world has nothing to do with looking toward an impossible utopian vision of society. But defeating the triple evils that King deplored is not utopian. It is certainly part of the kingdom of God, and King believed that it was possible even in this life. Francis agrees, as we see in his writings, and certainly in his 2015 address. Dreaming, like nonviolence and love, is not passive. It may involve theoretical ideas and ideals, but it requires even more work to make the dreams a reality. For the Church to become an antiracist institution, every member must act with the soul force that King endorsed in his own life. For some of us, it means to teach, write, and educate ourselves. For others, it may mean activism on the ground. For still others, the only recourse will be civil disobedience and perhaps time in prison. But even though there is one Spirit, there are many gifts. Now, I turn to another great American, who also utilized the Spirit's gifts to work for a more loving society: Dorothy Day.

Chapter Three

DOROTHY DAY AND ENVIRONMENTAL PERSONALISM

> Without Dorothy, without that exemplary patience, courage, moral modesty, without this woman pounding at the locked door behind which the powerful mock the powerless with games of triage—without her, the resistance we have offered would be simply unthinkable. She urged our consciences off the beaten track; she made the impossible (in our case) probable, and then actual. She did this, first of all, by living as though the truth were true.
>
> —Daniel Berrigan, SJ[1]

The only woman whom Pope Francis cited in his 2015 address to Congress, Dorothy Day is a remarkable figure, arguably "the most significant, interesting, and influential person in the history of American Catholicism."[2] While there are certainly American Catholics who are more widely known to the general population of Americans (John F. Kennedy and Joe Biden, for starters), there are no American Catholics who impacted the landscape of the faith tradition on these shores more than Dorothy Day. As with the other three figures to whom

Pope Francis dedicated his address, Day is not easily catalogued. She certainly does not fit into one or another ideological category. While she was best known for a certain Christian variety of anarchism, she was simultaneously beholden to the Roman Catholic Church, even in some ways to the figures of the hierarchy. She never failed to abide by their earthly, ecclesial authority, or to write to them for assistance and prayers. Nevertheless, she did not place any sort of faith in these men that they would do what was most just in a given situation.[3] As the cofounder (with Peter Maurin) of the Catholic Worker movement on May 1, 1933, Day was the kind of bold cultural revolutionary that Francis calls us all to be in *Laudato Si'*.

This chapter examines Day's contribution to American Catholicism in three particular areas. The first area regards labor. Since Pope Leo XIII's 1891 promulgation of the encyclical *Rerum Novarum*, the rights of workers and the dignity of work itself has been foundational in the body of official Catholic social thought. But Day's intervention on work was even more radical than that of popes of her day and since. What relevance does this writing on work have in the larger context of the United States? What has been Pope Francis's own message regarding workers' rights? What overlap is there between the two? Finally, what does Day's message about the morality of labor say to American Catholicism today?

Next, I turn to Day's most infamous trait in her own life's work: pacifism. As with two of the other three figures that Francis mentions in his address, Day was committed to nonviolence. Furthermore, in the case of Day, Merton, and King, their relationship to nonviolence was directly influenced by the commandments of Jesus in the gospel. Like the other pacifists Francis mentions as great Americans, Day paid a great price for her approach to war and peace.[4] In the first three years of the Catholic Worker movement, there was enormous support for her efforts. But Day's failure to support Franco (contrary to most Catholics throughout the world) in the Spanish Civil War caused massive fallout.[5] This tension within the movement, however, did not convince Day that she was wrong, and the Catholic Worker movement ultimately followed her example: "Despite closed houses, division among co-workers, and lost subscriptions, Dorothy's view—shared by many—prevailed."[6] For her part, Day became the signal figure of Catholic pacifism in the United States during the twentieth century. But Francis does not mention Day's position on nonviolence in his address, so it is worth asking: What role should Day's pacifism play in analyzing her classification as one of his great Americans?

Third and finally, I turn to a topic that Francis does mention while extoling Day during his address: the environment. Even though Day's years at the helm of the Catholic Worker predate Francis's encyclical by decades, her own priorities (along with those of her colleague Peter Maurin) parallel those of Francis. What Peter Maurin termed the *Green Revolution* was at the heart of the Catholic Worker movement. As such, it meant that the Catholic Worker community would be based not only in the cities, but also would require a move to farms, or what Maurin referred to as "agronomic universities." In bringing about such a revolution, their hope was that "a return to the land could mitigate the technological and cyclical unemployment...inherent in an industrial economy. Moreover, subsistence farming and crafts centered the forces of production once again on need rather than profit, and so provided a basis for recovering the value of cooperation and the spiritual dimension of human existence."[7] While many analyses of Day's life may overlook this "Green Revolution," no analysis of Francis's pontificate can adequately take stock of his legacy without grappling with *Laudato Si'* and his treatment of the natural environment. Now, in the address, Francis links his own legacy with Day's importance in American Catholicism. Truth be told, as Day's cause for canonization inches toward completion in the coming years, Francis has called our attention in this address to the fact that Day will be a patron saint of peacemaking, workers, and ecology; and indeed, of the United States.

Dorothy Day and Work

Of the many groups of people who were adversely affected by the COVID-19 pandemic, workers in some sectors have often gone overlooked. At the height of the unemployment crisis in this pandemic, 14.8 percent of Americans were out of work. While that number has dipped, the economic reality of COVID-19 will likely be felt for a long time to come. During the darkest days of the pandemic, the daily reports of infections, hospitalizations, and deaths were accompanied every Thursday by the newest unemployment data. Even though they might be healthy, these people did not know what they would do for work, how they would pay their rent, or how they would feed their children.

Of course, Catholic social teaching does not overlook workers; labor and workers' rights are at the very ground level of modern Catholic social encyclicals. In *Rerum Novarum*, Pope Leo XIII notes a number of core realities in any discussion of the rights of workers.[8] He considers things such as the care for workers' souls (no. 32), working hours (no. 33), protection of young children from onerous work (no. 33), the just wage (no. 34), and the benefits of accruing private property for oneself and one's family (no. 35). These are all inescapable parts of workers' rights in Catholic social thought. Few American Catholics have embraced this principle more than Dorothy Day. I examine how Day's insights complement Francis's writings on labor;[9] I suggest a renewal of activism in the Church on behalf of workers based on the words and actions of Pope Francis and Dorothy Day; and I consider Day's role in the Communion of Saints as a patron of workers.

Day and Francis on Labor

To think of Dorothy Day is to think, even if subconsciously, of the Catholic Worker. Therefore, it is an inescapable reality of Day's life to think of work and workers. As you might expect, she frequently addressed the topic in her many writings, itself a form of work. As she writes in *The Long Loneliness*, "*The Catholic Worker*, as the name implied, was directed to the worker, but we used the word in its broadest sense, meaning those who worked with hand or brain, those who did physical, mental or spiritual work. But we thought primarily of the poor, the dispossessed, the exploited."[10] To be sure, the vast majority of Day's life was given over to the poor and discernment of how best to be at their service. Similarly, Pope Francis himself has often called for a "poor church for the poor."[11] In fact, these words were among the very first that entered his thoughts as he was elected pope. What is the common link between Day's and Francis's affirmation of the Catholic social doctrine of the preferential option for the poor? I submit that it is the person of Jesus. As Day writes of this example,

His teaching transcended all the wisdom of the scribes and
pharisees, and taught us the most effective means of living
in this world while preparing for the next. And He directed
His sublime words to the poorest of the poor, to the people

who thronged the towns and followed after John the Baptist, who hung around, sick and poverty-stricken at the doors of the rich man.[12]

Even if we often do not see the tragedies of worker maltreatment, they are part of the daily reality that countless people experience throughout the world. For instance, on April 24, 2013, in Dhaka, Bangladesh, the Rana Plaza garment factory collapsed, killing 1,134 human beings who worked and lived within it and injuring 2,000 more. The disaster, a tragic event in itself, uncovered many other tragedies that were part of the operations at this factory even before this horrible moment. "About 3.6 million people work in Bangladesh's garment industry, making it the world's second-largest apparel exporter behind China. The industry employs mostly women, some of whom earn as little as $38 a month."[13] Only a week later, on the Feast of St. Joseph the Worker, May 1, 2013, Pope Francis reflected on this event and called for an end to slave labor. Furthermore, in his homily, he noted the close connection between Jesus and labor: "Work is very, very, very evangelical."[14] The victims of the Dhaka garment factory collapse were thrown away by society long before the day they died; they were casualties of a consumer society that does not care for its workers. We've read Matthew 25 enough times to know who was killed that day. Even if Jesus ought to be the backbone of Catholic social doctrine on labor, what sets apart figures such as Day and Francis is that they frequently cite his example when explaining the rights of workers. Both Day and Francis take Jesus as their motivation in calling for justice for the poor.

Dorothy Day was also no stranger to worker injustice and maltreatment. She constantly reflected on this issue as she penned her own writings, and more importantly, carried out genuine works of mercy in her houses of hospitality. In her column of December 1946, Day addressed the coal workers' strike that was taking place at the time. She informs her readers that the reasons for the western Pennsylvania coal miners' strike were many, including a lack of reasonable working hours. Moreover, Day writes, "It is about the welfare fund. Up to this time there have been no pensions, no recreation, no education, no adequate medical services. The need for such a fund is evidenced by these figures: Every year some 1,500 miners are killed; some 60,000 to 70,000 are injured, many of them so badly they are thrown on the scrap heap."[15] Or, as Francis has constantly said since his election as pope, there is a "throwaway culture" that we must overcome (see *Laudato Si'* 16, 22, 43, 123).

Both Day and Francis present a christocentric message in their writings on labor, yet it is a message that remains fundamentally practical and clearsighted. As Day wrote in 1947,

> It is indeed hard to see Christ in the undeserving poor, in His most degraded guise. We admit that there will always be the poor, the wastrel, the drunk, the sinner. But Christ came to save them. He loved them. We just insist that there do not need to be so many of them, the degraded, the twisted, the warped, the miserable ones, employed and unemployed.[16]

At the very heart of Day's ethic is the belief that all human beings are created in the image and likeness of God. Jesus's ethic was instructive for everything that the Catholic Worker movement would carry out in its daily activities. These activities were done sometimes in the face of more passive approaches on the part of the majority of Catholics. Of these Catholics, Day recounts, "They were our own, and we reacted sharply to the accusation that when it came to private morality the Catholics shone but when it came to social and political morality, they were often conscienceless."[17] The same chasm is readily seen today, especially in this country, and particularly in the wake of the election of the second Catholic president, when many bishops are ready to engage in cultural warfare by denying the reception of the Eucharist to any politician who supports abortion rights while never mentioning the same consequence for a Catholic in public life who supports the death penalty or, to the point of this chapter, fails to pay their employees just wages.

And yet, Day realized that even these efforts fell short of the Christian call to holiness:

> Breadlines are not enough; hospices are not enough. I know we will always have men on the road. But we need communities of work, land for the landless, true farming communes, cooperatives and credit unions. There is much that is wild, prophetic, and holy about our work—it is that

which attracts the young who come to help us. But the heart hungers for that new social order wherein justice dwelleth.[18]

Or, as Pope Francis would say, there needs to be a "bold cultural revolution" (*Laudato Si'* 114). How do we bring about this revolution in the Church and society today? It is to this question that I turn next.

Ecclesial Activism and Labor

Francis has already hinted at one way to carry out this bold cultural revolution. In the same document in which he calls for this radical movement, he calls our attention to the monastic tradition of prayer and work (*ora et labora*), observing that for St. Benedict and his brethren, "Seeing manual labor as spiritually meaningful proved revolutionary" (*Laudato Si'* 126). Basically, what Francis implies in calling for such revolution is that the Church itself has grown stagnant; instead of being revolutionary, it has been complacent and satisfied with the status quo. This cannot be what the Church is about if it is to carry out the gospel authentically. Moreover, it is exactly the opposite of what Dorothy Day stood for in her own life and daily works of mercy. Because Day frequently invoked the Catholic social tradition as it was unfolding in her own time, it would be helpful to do the same today with Francis's own magisterial teachings. Here, I present three concrete steps that can spring from activism in the Church (but not be limited to Church structures) that can bring about the revolution for which Pope Francis is advocating.

As Christine Firer Hinze has observed, "The early twentieth century Catholic Church had little reputation for social progressivism, much less radicalism. Still Pope Leo XIII's 1891 brief on the condition of labor had ushered the Church into a new type of public engagement, in which its criticisms of the economic status quo were clear and prominent."[19] It is almost an understatement today to say that in the early twenty-first century, the Catholic Church remains an institution that is not well known for its "social progressivism, much less radicalism." But if, as Hinze points out, the Church is involved in this new type of public economic engagement, why does it still have such a reputation? The answer is because the Church does not engage in economic issues with as much vigor or passion as it does in issues of sexual morality.[20] This was not always the case. One example will help us point to the first two ecclesial steps toward worker justice today: widespread education in Catholic social teaching and official support for striking workers.

The example to which I allude is that of César Chávez and the California farmworkers. It is telling that until President Joe Biden placed a bust of Chávez behind his desk in the Oval Office in January 2021, many U.S. Catholics were unfamiliar with Chávez. Just decades before Biden took office, Chávez was a renowned figure in American Catholicism. Along with Dolores Huerta, Chávez founded the National Farm Workers Association (NFWA) in 1962, after having been introduced to Catholic social teaching a decade earlier by Donald McDonnell, "a San Francisco priest who worked as part of a mission team serving migrant field workers."[21]

Pope Francis also maintains that education is not only important in terms of passing on the Church's social teaching, but in educating one in work itself. In an address to the Movement of Christian Workers, he stated, "Educating is a great vocation: as St. Joseph trained Jesus in the art of carpentry, you too are called to help the younger generations to discover the beauty of truly human work."[22] Before one can enact any principle of Catholic social teaching, they must have an actual teacher to impart to them what the Church teaches about this or that particular issue. Likewise, before an individual begins work, someone must teach them how to do it. Without teachers, we are left with dispiriting questions: What would have happened if Father McDonnell had never shared Catholic social principles with Chávez? Only after Catholic social teaching is effectively handed on can it be implemented. This first requires an educational program so that Catholic social teaching will no longer be "the Church's best-kept secret." It ought to be taught in Catholic schools and in CCD courses, along with the major figures in the tradition such as Chávez and Day. It should be preached on frequently from the pulpit; excerpts of encyclicals could be included in bulletin inserts each week. There should be an easy way to find information on CST on diocesan and parish webpages, and it should be constantly shared through various social media accounts. César Chávez ought to be a well-known American Catholic figure once again.

The second of these steps is official support for labor witnesses from Church leaders. Chávez's support from the bishops in the 1960s was mixed. As James Fisher notes, "In 1965, the NFWA joined a strike against table grape growers in Delano, California, that had been launched by a largely Filipino-American agricultural workers union. In the course of the five-year strike the two groups merged to form the United Farm Workers [UFW] Association."[23] In this case, though, the United States Catholic bishops played a major role as mediators.[24] As Charles Curran explains, "Two significant pro-grower bishops in California prevented the bishops from endorsing the boycott, and the bishops compromised by setting up a mediation."[25] By 1972, during a later strike of the UFW against the lettuce growers in the Salinas Valley, even the two bishops who had held out two years earlier had since come to support Chávez and the strikers. In this case, it was "the Committee on Social Development of the bishops' conference—but not the entire body of bishops [who] supported a boycott of lettuce not harvested by the UFW."[26] While the bishops have certainly supported labor rights such as those the UFW fought for in 1972, they have not done so with the same passion and vigor with which they oppose abortion. What would be a more revolutionary type of witness? For this, I turn to the third and boldest example.

Pope Francis cannot help but see a clear connection between the plight of workers and the economic destruction caused by war. This is a good moment to recall that Francis, like Dorothy Day, sees the close interrelation of various social injustices. Francis has frequently lamented that human beings worship money rather than God, and consequently, human beings and other living creatures are discarded without any care for their well-being. Francis has said that one of the reasons for this is that "indifference has been globalized."[27] One of the saddest realities we are seeing, especially in the United States today, is that *indifference has also been ecclesialized.* In other words, members of our churches, including the hierarchy, have largely forgotten those who labor and receive so few benefits. This sin cries out to heaven. It is not enough merely to say that workers deserve certain rights if dioceses, parishes, universities, and groups of Catholics will not support them in tangible ways. This leads me to one such tangible response.

I suggest that Dorothy Day's own example is a wonderful model for the bishops. While the aforementioned committee did support the boycott, Day took it a step further, engaging in active civil disobedience, which is the third step I recommend here. Since the California Jurisdictional Strike Act was interpreted as prohibiting strikes and boycotts, all of this activity was deemed illegal.[28] Chávez had already been jailed in defiance of this law. Day, standing in the long line of support for the farm workers, traveled to California to aid what became known as *La Causa* because of her significant presence. As her biographer Jim Forest noted, "The first *Catholic Worker* article on the plight of farm workers appeared in 1934....For more than a decade beginning in 1965, it was a rare issue which failed to speak about the farm workers' struggle to unionize themselves."[29] Despite her frail health, Day's 1973 sojourn in California would provide one of the lasting images of her life, possibly the most famous photograph ever snapped of her. The picture, which is venerated by peace and labor groups, and adorns at least one edition of *The Long Loneliness*, is of an elderly woman sitting in a chair-cane, being confronted by police officers about to arrest her.[30] The cause? Solidarity with the farm workers. Perhaps this is the type of image Philip Berrigan had in mind when he said, "Your hope is where your ass is."[31] In this picture, Day is sitting, placing her body squarely in an uncomfortable place. Though seated, she was taking a stand with Chávez and the farm workers. As Chávez wrote in a tribute to Day after her death, she was but the most famous of a larger group: "And Dorothy came to be with us in Fresno, along with nearly a hundred priests and nuns and lay people. The picture that was taken of her that day, sitting amongst the strikers and the police, is a classic portrayal of her internal peace and strength in the midst of turmoil and conflict."[32]

Pope Francis is abundantly clear on this front. Recently, there has been much discussion in the United States about how the Catholic bishops of the country do not follow Francis's action items.[33] Hear what he says about workers' dignity and rights: "Every injustice inflicted on a person who works tramples on human dignity; and also the dignity of the one who does this injustice. It lowers the level and we end up with that tension that exists between a dictator and a slave."[34] So, inspired by Day's famous photograph and seated witness of solidarity, we are left to wonder today at the literal and metaphorical locations of the U.S. bishops' chairs. Where are their *cathedras*? In fact, we hardly have to wonder at all. Sadly, they seem to be largely in churches, chanceries, and even worse, the politicians' offices.[35] Pope Francis's ultimate aim is in line with Catholic social teaching since *Rerum Novarum*: the economy is meant to serve human beings, not vice versa. Pope Francis has said that failing to protest the throwaway culture in which we live is a sure sign of narcissism.[36] Some of the issues we might protest for in public, especially as university communities in the Catholic tradition, are those recently catalogued by Christine Firer Hinze: living wages, reduction of financial burdens and providing of resources, universal basic income, prioritizing productive and fairly remunerated work, and businesses serving the common good, among many other issues.[37]

Dorothy Day as the Patron Saint of Workers

How would Dorothy Day live during COVID-19? Perhaps more importantly, how would she live in a post-COVID world? These questions are quite apt for our current moment. It might seem that my three suggestions for activism in the previous section are not nearly optimistic enough. And yet, without accomplishing all three of them, we will inevitably fall short of the bold cultural revolution to which Pope Francis has called us. To be truthful, I must admit that I am more than a bit pessimistic in thinking that the Church in the United States may be capable of an about-face on being revolutionary when it comes to fighting for workers' rights. And yet, there is reason for hope. In this section, I turn to Dorothy Day's cause for canonization, which is underway. The debate over whether or not she ought to be considered a saint has been perennial in Catholic left circles over the past decades.[38] But she is the perfect figure for this particular discussion because she is a bridge between the United States Catholic bishops and those radicals who venerate her legacy. Regardless of whether or not certain individuals on the Catholic left believe Day should be a candidate for canonization, they revere her for her integrity of life. The U.S. bishops showed in their 2012 Annual Fall Assembly that they were enthusiastic about Day's cause for canonization moving forward and they also lauded her for her holiness.

In the Catholic tradition, St. Joseph has been venerated as the patron saint of workers. I believe that once Day is canonized, she ought to take on that mantle. (And clearly, St. Joseph is a patron for Day as well, since one of the Catholic Worker houses in Manhattan is named after him.) We should strive to make Day's prayer our own: "Raise up more and more leader-servants throughout the country to stand with Cesar Chavez in this nonviolent struggle with Mammon, in all the rural districts of North and South…wherever men, women, and children work on the land. Help make a new order wherein justice flourishes."[39] But more than that, we should ask for her intercession that those entrusted with leadership in the Church take that mantle seriously when it comes to protecting and promoting justice for all workers, whether in the fields, the parish office, or whatever line of work in which they are employed. We should pray unceasingly for Day's aid for those of us who are leaders in colleges and universities. What can we do to make labor more just in our own backyards? While we may not all be in administrative roles, we have particular positions of responsibility on our campuses, not only with our students, but with the wider community. Especially if we work at Catholic institutions that profess some allegiance to magisterial teaching, it is incumbent upon us to work for a more just reality among our colleagues. What are our custodial and maintenance staff being paid? Do they have benefits? How many hours are they working? Was anyone laid off during the COVID-19 pandemic? Were they reinstated when operations returned to normal?[40]

If the answers to any of those questions indict our institutions, then they also indict Catholic theologians who are their colleagues. Writing as such a person, I wonder how we can take ourselves seriously if we do not come to support their cause. Pope Francis has employed a commentary on Genesis 11 and the story of the Tower of Babel to illustrate this point:

> According to the rabbi, if a brick fell it was a great tragedy: work stopped and the negligent worker was beaten severely as an example. But if a worker fell to his death? The work went one. One of the surplus laborers—slaves waiting in line for work—stepped forward to take his place so that the tower could continue to rise.[41]

We might say today that this sounds awful; we would never do that. And yet, if a part-time professor in our department suddenly drops a class, we are all too eager to sign up another individual at a moment's notice to work for a pittance. We need to carry out a revolution on behalf of fair remuneration for all workers at the university level. To quote again from Francis, "Either a society is geared to a culture of sacrifice—the triumph of the fittest and the throwaway culture—or to mercy and care. People or bricks: it is time to choose."[42] Through the intercession of Dorothy Day, let us choose mercy and care. For the love of God, let us choose people.

Dorothy Day the Pacifist

There was no greater promoter of peace in twentieth-century American Catholicism than Day. I can think of no greater model for the renewed evangelical effort in the Church. In particular, this section argues that the Church can authentically utilize Day in the twenty-first century as a means of promoting peace in a pluralistic world. First, I discuss Day as an instrumental catalyst for the writing of *Pacem in Terris*, which was a watershed document in the history of the Church. Second, I present the few citations from Day's own writings on that encyclical letter, which provide a glimpse into her understanding of the relationship between the successor of St. Peter and the movement for peace in the world. Third, and finally, I return to the understanding of Day as the model of the "New Evangelizer" and ponder how the Church may take on her example of sainthood for the entire world. I argue that this model has ramifications beyond any single group of people. It is important for every sector of Catholicism and should be shared with other Christian denominations and other faith traditions.

In the years leading up to the promulgation of *Pacem in Terris* on April 11, 1963, Dorothy Day had already cemented herself as a major figure in the Roman Catholic Church in the United States. As Mel Piehl puts it, "The Catholic Worker—and therefore American Catholic radicalism—was Dorothy Day's invention, and she pervaded its history for so long that a social, religious, and intellectual history of American Catholic radicalism up to 1965 turns out to be, in significant measure, an interpretation of the social outlook, religion, and ideas of this one person."[43] Drew Christiansen has helpfully reminded us that while *Pacem in Terris* was being written, "the cold war was at its height. In March [1962] the Berlin Wall went up. In October, just as Vatican II began, the United States and the Soviet Union came to the brink of nuclear war over the deployment of Soviet missiles in Cuba."[44] It is clear from the message of the encyclical that John XXIII wished to turn a new page in the history of the Catholic understanding of war and peace. Furthermore, he makes it clear that he is referring to the specific problem brought about by modern weaponry: "In an age such as ours which prides itself on its atomic energy it is contrary to reason to hold that war is now a suitable way to restore rights which have been violated" (*Pacem in Terris* 127). Here Pope John opens the door for the fathers of Vatican II to declare that conscientious objection to warfare is, indeed, a viable option for Catholics, to be upheld in union with the just war theory. Moreover, he is also implicitly hearkening to the many actions for peace that Dorothy Day had organized in the decades preceding the encyclical. John makes it a point to "exhort our children to take an active part in public life, and to contribute toward the attainment of the common good of the entire human family as well as to that of their own country" (no. 146). Clearly, this exhortation has been something that American Catholics have taken quite seriously in the decades since the promulgation of this encyclical. But for Day and her disciples, it was nothing new. As Jim Forest reminds us, "As early as July 1935, just two years after Hitler had become chancellor of Germany, opposition to his anti-Semitic policies had led the Catholic Worker community in New York to the docks on Manhattan's Upper West Side to join in picketing a German liner."[45] Let us not forget that this action itself was a full twenty-eight years before Pope John issued his clarion call to Catholics and all people of the world for greater action in public life for the common good of all.

Any number of devil's advocates in the case of Dorothy Day (or any absolute pacifist for that matter) always point to what many call the last "good war"—World War II—when challenging the absolute pacifist position that all warfare is immoral. For Day and the minority of the Workers who staunchly defended pacifism during World War II, it was not an either/or choice between pacifism and protection of the Jewish people. For Day, both of these positions were a part of the common good that Pope John called all people to work toward in *Pacem in Terris*. In a letter to the New York City police commissioner, written as a response to the violence the police force used against the protesters at the aforementioned event, Day contends, "As Catholics we too feel called upon to protest against the Nazi persecution of Catholics and Jews by demonstration and distribution of literature. We feel that we would be neglecting our duty as Catholics if we did not do this."[46] At the same time, Day certainly felt that her duty as a Catholic also extended to the realm of nonviolence. She felt there was no tension between opposing Nazism and simultaneously opposing American involvement in World War II. In the January 1942 edition of the *Catholic Worker*, Day writes, "We are still pacifists. Our manifesto is the Sermon on the Mount, which means that we will try to be peacemakers. Speaking for many of our conscientious objectors, we will not participate in armed warfare or in making munitions, or by buying government bonds to prosecute the war, or in urging others to these efforts."[47] Only four months later, Day would admit that she had been accused of killing the Catholic Worker movement because of her strict adherence to a pacifist stance.

It is interesting to note the shift in the official teaching of the Catholic Church in the area of conscientious objection to warfare that took place in the course of Day's writing and prophetic activism. As recently as the 1956 Christmas radio address of Pope Pius XII, the pontiff had ruled out conscientious objection as a viable moral stance for a Catholic to take up.[48] Since this ban on conscientious objection to warfare had been the party line of the Church all throughout World War II, we would do well to remember that, as Patricia McNeal notes, "it was the Catholic Worker movement alone, among all American Catholic groups, that offered assistance to individuals who conscientiously objected to World War II."[49] With the promulgation of *Pacem in Terris*, there was some confusion among theologians as to whether or not Pope John had abolished the just war theory. In fact, he hadn't even abolished Pius XII's ban on conscientious objection. Through this confusion, however, he opened the door for further consideration of war during Vatican II. Along those lines, *Gaudium et Spes* declares, "It seems right that laws make humane provisions for the case of those who for reasons of conscience refuse to bear arms" (no. 79). This statement was prefigured in *Pacem in Terris*, and Dorothy Day was certainly a catalyst for that encyclical through her own prophetic and courageous support for conscientious objectors to World War II. As Jim Forest remarks, *Pacem in Terris*'s "spirit and principles had long been anticipated by Dorothy."[50]

Proposition 31 of the 2012 meeting of the Synod of Bishops on the New Evangelization is especially pertinent regarding Day: "New Evangelization and the Option for the Poor."[51] As we know, it was part of Day's legacy that she spent so much of herself serving the poor that she and her movement became synonymous with life in poverty. In *Pacem in Terris*, Pope John implies what is now obvious: the poor will suffer disproportionately from nuclear weapons. He states that since it is only the wealthiest countries building up their nuclear arsenals, "while the people of these countries are loaded with heavy burdens, other countries as a result are deprived of the collaboration they need in order to make economic and social progress" (*Pacem in Terris* 109). As Day puts it, the commitment to the poor also has to be one on which the Christian stakes her life: "Whatever we can do to combat these widespread social evils [of poverty] by combating their causes we must do. But above all the responsibility is a personal one. The message we have been given comes from the Cross."[52] The cross, as Pope Francis has shown clearly, is also intimately connected to all of creation, which is being crucified today. It is to this sin that I now turn.

Dorothy Day and the Green Revolution

Though her name does not appear in the text or notes of *Laudato Si'*, the keen observer of papal writings and the history of the Catholic Worker movement can see Day's influence all over the encyclical that was written "On Care for Our Common Home." Even if the Green Revolution was the brainchild of Peter Maurin (as were many other core tenets of the Catholic Worker movement), Day's life and writings illuminate it, which is part of the reason that she rose to such prominence among American Catholics. Day's close association with the land predated Pope Francis's attention to the natural environment by many decades, and her turn to the land presents us with a challenge and a way to see a major connection between various social injustices. Like King, Day espoused a worldview wherein the many social injustices that we face are linked together by common features. It is impossible to separate polluting the earth from racism, for example.[53] In this final, brief section of the chapter, I turn to the passages Francis cites from *Laudato Si'* in his address, while discussing Day as a great American who laid the groundwork for this encyclical on care for creation.

While no papal document can be reduced to three words, the phrase *everything is connected* echoes in the minds of anyone who has read *Laudato Si'*.[54] It is a clarion call from Francis that we cannot compartmentalize our lives into neat sections so that different facets of our existence, either as individuals or groups, can remain disparate. In other words, everything makes up the integral whole. "Human ecology" and "environmental ecology" come together in integral ecology. This comes out most clearly when Francis declares that human ecology shows forth "the relationship between human life and the moral law, which is inscribed in our nature and is necessary for the creation of a more dignified environment" (*Laudato Si'* 155). Put another way, human ecology is a pathway to integral ecology. Francis continues,

"It is enough to recognize that our body itself establishes us in a direct relationship with the environment and with other living beings" (no. 155).[55]

In lauding Day, Francis calls for us to "redirect our steps" (no. 61), clearly acknowledging that the steps we have been taking as a people have not been in accordance with ethical living and following the gospel. Day is a helpful figure to mention in this regard because she, like many other key figures, went through a conversion experience. Not only did Day convert to Catholicism,[56] but she also realized that each individual is called to go through a conversion on a daily basis; we are called not to be stagnant or remain in the status quo with our faith but must constantly renew it. Francis makes clear that one of the most obvious ways to go through a conversion today is through the means of an ecological conversion (*Laudato Si'* 216–21). Day's understanding of conversion, though, is one that we are meant to take on today. Just as when we go from hatred to loving acceptance, from a closed mind to an open mind, from violence to nonviolence, Pope Francis is asking us to convert our ways from unsustainability to sustainability. Francis calls for an end to "tyrannical anthropocentrism" (no. 68). How can one maintain personalism as Day does, and turn from this worldview?

One of the foremost proponents of personalism in the Catholic intellectual tradition, Jacques Maritain, explains that in a personalist society, the goal is to "see the mark of human dignity first and foremost in the power to make [the]…goods of nature serve the common conquest of intrinsically human, moral, and spiritual goods and of man's freedom of autonomy."[57] But reading personalism too narrowly can present a serious danger of not giving "enough importance to the many aspects of human existence."[58] In summarizing Louis Janssens's personalist criterion, Richard Gula writes, "An action is morally right if it is beneficial to the person adequately considered in himself or herself…and in his or her relations (i.e., to others, to social structures, to *the material world*, and to God)."[59] In light of this thinking, Bernard Brady has gone so far as to conclude, "It would not be incorrect to say that the fundamental idea underlying contemporary Catholic social thought is personalism."[60] Personalism, likewise, has been at the very heart of the Catholic Worker movement since its founding. It was the philosophical grounding for the movement's closeness to the gospel and its insistence on fulfilling the works of mercy in their daily lives. For Day, personalism meant that each individual ought to have a sense of responsibility for every other person with whom they interacted. Moreover, taking the criterion enumerated above, each individual ought to recognize her responsibility to the entire planet. If Francis calls us to a "bold cultural revolution," Day believed the basis for that revolution must be personalist.[61] Authentic personalism must be environmental personalism.[62]

Authentic personalism, in the mode of Dorothy Day and Peter Maurin, must return to care for all creation. In fact, as Francis Sicius writes, "Maurin did not often use the word personalism. Rather he referred to a 'Green Revolution,' which called for humanity to live in closer harmony with each other and their natural environment."[63] As Francis cited from *Laudato Si'* in his address, the ecological and personalist conversion to which we are called will mean utilizing technology in a much different way than we currently do. It is likely that Maurin, for his part at least, would be too extreme in this regard according to Francis's standards. Day reminds us that Maurin "cried out against the machine."[64] While Francis clearly sees the limited advantages of technology, it is not as clear that Day and Maurin would advocate the same. How can we move beyond that impasse?

For one potential means of finding common ground here, I turn to the confidence Francis voiced in his address for "America's outstanding academic and research institutions." There is certainly some irony that Francis included this piece of encouragement in the Day section of his address since there is a longstanding tension between the Catholic Worker and academia. There are many reasons for such a break between the liberal center and the radicalism of the Worker.[65] That reality notwithstanding, it is an inescapable fact that the Catholic Worker movement itself has never been anti-intellectual.[66] Day's writings themselves are worthy of academic study.[67] If there is a tension between the Catholic Worker and Catholic higher education in the United States, there is also a paradoxical reality in Day herself:

> Dorothy Day herself was sometimes hard on lukewarm Christianity, and she was especially disdainful of those who "prematurely canonized" her in order to celebrate Christian ideals they were unwilling to live out. There was no way, she believed, to avoid the personal cost of genuine religiosity. Yet Day's vision of the Gospel was broad enough to accept a diversity of Christian vocations.[68]

Any Catholic intellectual who takes their faith and their profession seriously has to grapple with these words. In particular, those many scholars who have studied Day's life and witness must feel personally indicted by Day's own position here. What good is it to know about Christ, but not to act like him? This is the perennial challenge for every Catholic scholar, regardless of their field of expertise.

And yet, there is still an impasse between the academic community and the Catholic Worker community. How can we bridge that chasm? How can the agronomic universities and the traditional universities come together? We can start by a mutual commitment to the Green Revolution. Catholic colleges and universities ought to take seriously Pope Francis's call to disengage with the bad habits that continue to bring ruin to the planet. By word and action, they can educate their students in ecological ethics and stop investing in fossil fuels. They can "go green" by installing solar panels. But there is also a way in which the two communities—Catholic Worker and higher education—can come together. Catholic Workers can be speakers and guest lecturers in Catholic university classrooms, while university professors can be speakers at weekly clarification of thought meetings at Catholic Worker houses of hospitality. Both groups have people that are willing to make these connections because even though Catholic Workers and Catholic intellectuals represent small groups of the Catholic community, there are some that understand the tradition is based off the principle of "both-and." This is the very principle that enlightened Day's own thinking on the variety of vocations in the Church and world.

Chapter Four

THOMAS MERTON: AMERICAN MONASTICISM OR MONASTIC AMERICANISM?

Merton forged for himself a sophisticated and rich spiritual identity that spoke meaningfully to many others engaged in precisely the same task of welding together an identity made up of three seemingly disjunctive terms: "modern," "American," and "Catholic."

—Mark Massa, SJ[1]

When word had reached the United States that the celebrity priest, Thomas Merton, or Brother Louis as he was known in religious life, had died of an accidental electrocution in Bangkok, Thailand, on December 10, 1968, speculation arose about the multivalence of the event itself. But, as Paul Elie notes, "in that year of grandiose acts, of blood and fire, it was a spasm of direct and terrible experience, with no significance outside itself."[2] And yet Merton's death was very significant,

71

or at least as significant as the death of any signal figure can be in the life of a community. For the community of American Catholics in the years immediately following World War II, no Catholic writer had been more widely read than Merton. He was the muse of American Catholicism, and he wrote from a cloistered abbey, to boot! Like Day, Merton was a convert to Catholicism, and it may be that this identity— one marked by religious conversion—tells much of what Francis wants to convey about their experiences. In fact, it is worth noting that none of the four great Americans that Francis commends to us were cradle Catholics; two were Protestant (if one could even call Lincoln a Protestant). So "Catholic" is not a prerequisite for Francis's style of "greatness," though certainly there are many aspects of the Catholic faith as witnessed by Day and Merton that directed their steps in a way that Francis celebrates. In the previous chapter, I briefly mentioned the importance of conversion for Day. Conversion is an essential part of being a great American in Francis's view. In this chapter, I consider in more detail Merton's conversion, not only (or even primarily) in terms of religion, but rather his daily conversion to become more authentically himself.

Conversion, of course, need not be from one religious tradition (or none) to another. Rather, as Francis himself has taught, "Christian conversion demands reviewing especially those areas and aspects of life 'related to the social order and the pursuit of the common good'" (*Evangelii Gaudium* 182).[3] Therefore, conversion is part of the daily life of the believer. Or, in the words of Walter Conn, conversion can be "a cognitive, affective, moral, and faith transformation which a new and vital relationship with the person of Christ effects."[4] This chapter will examine what daily conversion might look like through the lens of Merton's life and writings. I will go about this in three sections. First, I reexamine one of Merton's most famous lines through the lens of Francis's address and our own experience of the global community today. In particular, I deal with the fraught notion of loving God, what that may entail, and what experiences it might elicit. In the second section, I return to a term I quickly sketched in chapter 1: *pontifex*. If Lincoln was a political bridge builder, then Merton was the interreligious bridge builder par excellence. How can we follow in his footsteps and engage in this type of dialogue today? In some ways the world is more open to this type of dialogue, and in other important ways, the culture does not allow for it. What can we do? Third, and finally, this chapter puts an Ignatian spin on Merton. In examining Lincoln, I argued that Francis leaned heavily on his Ignatian roots and the Contemplation to Attain Divine Love in formulating his understanding of political love. Similarly, in this chapter, I look to Ignatian spirituality to contend that Merton is one of the best public examples we have ever had for yet another Ignatian principle: contemplation and action. Many people consider these terms mutually exclusive. Ignatius's insights into the spiritual life have shown that they need not be, and in fact, if they are, then whichever element is present is crippled by the absence of its complement. In some ways, Merton is the most enigmatic figure among the four that Francis named in his address. That seems obvious since he was the only one who was a monk and had his own hermitage, choices that resonate as enigmatic in broader American culture. But in other ways, his elusiveness has nothing to do with his religious vows. Like Lincoln and King, Merton met an untimely death. Unlike them, though, he was not the victim of an assassin's bullet. Like all three of Francis's other subjects, however, he died in the midst of a search. Let's join that search.

"Loving God, and Yet Hating Him"

Perhaps it struck some listeners as odd that Francis would cite Merton in his address. What was so American about being a monk? Even if Francis's inclusion of Merton was unexpected, it was all the more incredible that Francis cited from the very first paragraph of Merton's autobiography, *The Seven Storey Mountain*, in which Merton describes himself as one among many human beings who found themselves "loving God and yet hating Him; born to love Him, living instead in fear and hopeless self-contradictory hungers."[5] Why would a great American, especially a Catholic, ever hate God? Doesn't the *Catechism* teach us otherwise? What is the pope getting at by citing this passage? The interpretive lens through which to view this citation is the remainder of that paragraph of the pope's address. In those lines, he mentions four particular characteristics of Merton's life that commend him to us: he was a man of prayer, a great thinker, a man of dialogue, and a promoter of peace. Once we see Merton in this light, it becomes clearer what he meant when he referred to his hatred for God. Merton's entire life was one of seeking God's presence in the world and in his daily actions. This ought to be the experience of every Christian, which is why daily conversion is part of the Christian life. But a conversion to *what*? Hearkening back to the introduction of this volume, Merton believes that we all must be prophets. In a remarkable conclusion to his analysis of Alfred Delp's prison meditations, Merton writes,

> No one has a more solemn obligation to understand the true nature of man's predicament than he who is called to a life of special holiness and dedication. The priest, the religious, the lay leader must, whether he likes it or not, fulfill in the world the role of a prophet. If he does not face the anguish of being a true prophet, he must enjoy the carrion comfort of acceptance in the society of the deluded by becoming a false prophet and participating in their delusions.[6]

The first of the four prophetic elements of Merton's life that Francis considers is prayer. It is fascinating that one of the figures that played an oversized role in Francis's life was always his grandmother, whose influence he often cites. Like Francis, Merton had a particular veneration for his own grandmother, Gertrude Merton. Merton remembers that "she taught me the Lord's Prayer."[7] Once he entered the Monastery of Our Lady of Gethsemani in Kentucky, Merton's prayer life encompassed more than rote recitation of the Lord's Prayer, and yet that formative memory of his grandmother never left him. Even if he had already committed himself to a more substantial prayer life after his conversion to Catholicism, participating in the eucharistic liturgy and the Liturgy of the Hours, Merton was not prepared for what he would experience upon visiting Gethsemani during Holy Week of 1941: "No one will find it hard to conceive the impression made on a man thrown suddenly into a Trappist monastery at four o'clock in the morning, after the night office, as I was."[8]

Merton writes of something altogether foreign in contemporary society: "I felt the deep, deep silence of the night, and of peace, and of holiness enfold me like love, like safety."[9] When I was in college, like many young people who I now have the privilege to teach, I discovered some things for the first time in my life. One of these things was silence just as Merton described it. My own brushes with silence began with moments on a campus ministry retreat in the fall semester of 2004. But even those moments, which were never longer than an hour, tested my limits. From there, it meant trying to work silence into my daily routine, which included so many things that did not jibe with silence. In one of the chapels on campus at Fordham University (my alma mater), there was a mural of Jesus that took up the entire sanctuary wall. In that space, at that time, Merton's words rang true for me. As did his experience of feeling like a foreigner when I spent three days with the nuns of Carmel de la Paix monastery in Mazille, France, in the spring of 2007. I present this personal anecdote not in a self-serving way but to underline the point that Merton did not experience an interior life that was unique to him alone, but one that is open for all. I hope Merton was correct when he concluded, "If we fill our lives with silence, then we live in hope, and Christ lives in us and gives our virtues much substance."[10]

It should come as no surprise that the pope has also considered the importance of prayer in the Christian life. From May 6, 2020, until June 16, 2021, Francis devoted his weekly audiences to a series of catecheses on the topic of prayer.[11] These covered a wide variety of issues, many of which were similar to what Merton himself discusses in his own writing. What is especially poignant is an overlapping with regard to Holy Week. For his part, during his Holy Week 2021 general audience catechesis on prayer, Pope Francis also discussed the role of silence in the spiritual life, especially in the time of Holy Saturday.[12] Silence is so important in the life of the prophet because it allows her to reflect on what is most important in her life and in the life of the world at a given moment in time. One does not engage in prophetic acts at random, but rather does these acts only after discernment, which only takes place in the context of silence.[13] This is one type of contemplation.[14] Contemplation requires a detached attitude with regard to material goods. Even though this seems to be a prerequisite of the monastic life, Merton would claim that anyone capable of treating things with open hands is capable of being a contemplative: "The contemplative does not cease to *know* external objects. But he ceases to be *guided* by them. He ceases to depend on them. He ceases to treat them as ultimate."[15] Therefore, there is not a one-size-fits-all approach to the mystical life. Each individual person needs to discern the objects from which they must divest. Or, as Merton's biographer Michael Mott puts it, "It is the very nature of the mystic's journey that he or she must go alone. Where the landscape is always changing one needs advice and encouragement to fire courage—a map is the most useless of impediments."[16]

As Merton's opening lines of *The Seven Storey Mountain* remind us, however, his prayer was very human. Like the rest of us, Merton was prone to feeling moments in which prayer did not come easily.[17] In the last decade, there was widespread disbelief and confusion when Mother Teresa's journals were made public, revealing that she herself had experienced dry moments in her prayer over a period of many years. But in fact, as Pope Francis reminds us,

> all Godly men and women report not only the joy of prayer, but also the tediousness and fatigue it can bring: at times it is a difficult struggle to keep to the time and ways of praying. Some saints continued it for years without finding any satisfaction in it, without perceiving its usefulness. Silence, prayer and concentration are difficult exercises, and sometimes human nature rebels. We would rather be anywhere else in the world, but not there, in that church pew, praying. Those who want to pray must remember that faith is not easy, and sometimes it moves forward in almost total darkness, without points of reference. There are moments in the life of faith that are dark, and therefore some saints call this "the dark night," because we hear nothing. But I continue to pray.[18]

For both Merton and Francis, the primary prescription for spiritual aridity in prayer is simply perseverance.

Even if Merton's writings after his entrance into the monastery present him as a spiritual master, that was clearly not always the case in his life. Merton's conversion to Catholicism, which he covered so exhaustively in his autobiography, was, as James Fisher puts it, "a largely intellectual affair."[19] This means that Merton did not enter Catholic culture with blinders on. Rather, it means that he could see a synergism between being a Catholic and being an American, albeit one who did not fit in with any sort of status quo. As Mark Massa has noted, Merton's conversion and ultimate emergence on the literary scene in the United States was a turning point in American Catholicism: "Much of American Catholic life in both the nineteenth and twentieth centuries had been consumed with 'fitting in' and striving after bourgeoisie 'normalcy.' In answer to the charge of being outsiders in an overwhelmingly Protestant culture, Catholic intellectual and ecclesial leaders had sought to prove how thoroughly *American* their religious tradition was."[20] When Francis notes Merton's thought, he is really alluding to a reality about what religious life in the United States ought to be, and even more about the Catholic intellectual tradition. Because Catholicism is, in large part, defined by a "both-and" inclusivity that means embracing more than only one alternative, Merton's approach spoke to American Catholics in the middle of the twentieth century.

Even though Merton's own intellectual approach was crucial in his life and work, it was not the entire story. As Anne Carr suggests, Merton's "writing speaks to the need, felt by so many today, to explore a personal realm of experience that includes but goes beyond the intellectual and is sometimes spoken of as the realm of imagination, intuition, or wholeness. For Merton's is a contemplative theology that seeks to be radically experiential."[21] There are also dangers to this approach. One danger is that an individual becomes a walking contradiction. In Merton's case, the psychoanalyst Gregory Zilboorg diagnosed the problem as narcissism: "You want a hermitage in Times Square with a large sign over it saying 'HERMIT.'"[22] The other danger is an opposing view of Massa's proffered above: Merton's renunciation of his preconversion lifestyle could be seen not as a means of helping Catholic culture blend healthily with American culture, but rather as a countercultural challenge to the status quo.[23] The danger is not that there might be some areas when Catholic and American cultures clash, but rather that the Catholic culture be sectarian.[24] This was not Merton's approach. He believed that contemplation ought to be complemented by action. It is to that experiential and contemplative theology that I now turn.

Contemplation and Action: A Way Forward

When I first stepped foot in my Jesuit high school at the turn of the millennium, and again when I matriculated at Fordham University four years later, one of the very first catchphrases I heard was *contemplatives in action*. What was a contemplative? It quickly dawned on me that I had a great deal to learn, not just about Jesuit lingo, but about crucial terminology. In fact, it became painfully obvious that even my understanding of *action* was deficient, at least according to the standards of Christian spirituality. Even if the concept of contemplation in action has been co-opted by the Jesuits, perhaps no Catholic thinker has tackled the thorny issue with greater aplomb than Merton, a Trappist monk, who had seemingly fled the world. Or had he? Clearly Pope Francis had his reasons for numbering Merton among his great Americans. Having already briefly examined Merton's role as a thinker and an exegete of prayer, I move now to the relationship between contemplation and action and how that ought to manifest itself in the world, according to Merton: through concrete movement toward a world of peace.

Even though Merton decried the plague of global warfare and violence, he claimed not to be a pacifist.[25] Like Pope Francis, Merton believed that there were certain times when violence might be justified. And yet, Merton was one of the foremost voices for gospel nonviolence in the twentieth-century Catholic Church. He, along with Dorothy Day and Daniel Berrigan, vociferously argued for peace in the American Church in response to the Vietnam War. In fact, these individuals formed something of a troika in the turbulent days of the 1960s, when each had attained public notoriety. They each had a radical lifestyle that drew America's attention. Merton and Day were two adult converts to Catholicism who went to live out their new faith in different ways: one established a house of hospitality in Manhattan, and the other entered a cloistered monastery in Kentucky. As for Berrigan, he was a cradle Catholic who had entered the Jesuits right out of high school (as so many of his confreres did in the days before Vatican II) and became active in the antiwar movement, especially garnering attention for nonviolent civil disobedience. Despite their differences, what makes these three inseparable in American Catholic history is their literary output. Each of them was an author extraordinaire, writing some of the most interesting spiritual autobiographies of their time (or any time). All were also people of intense prayer. That prayer, even in the case of the monk, did not result in a spirituality that eschewed the world. Rather, all three of them emerged as *both* contemplative *and* active. In so being, they were very Catholic.

Merton was also a precursor to the just peace movement. In his virtue-based just peace ethic, Eli McCarthy argues that there are fourteen just peace practices.[26] While space does not permit me to analyze Merton through the lens of each of them, here I will select one from each category to show how Merton embodies these practices in his own thought.[27] First, the practice of sustaining spiritual practices is essential for Merton and, indeed, for any Catholic who is interested in being a contemplative in action. I have already briefly introduced Merton's understanding of contemplation, but it particularly resonated with the American Catholic's involvement in the world. In Merton's essay on this topic, after reflecting that monastic life reminds us of our collective past he writes, "Thus even into the confused activism of Western life is woven a certain memory of contemplation."[28] Notice here that Merton does not say "action," but "activism." The martyred Jesuit Ignacio Ella-curía puts it this way:

> The spiritual moment cannot be separated from the mis-sional; the moment of contemplation cannot be separated from the moment of action—as if the first ones were the truly spiritual moments and the second ones their mere results; as if the first were the place where God is encountered and the second the place where men and women are encountered. This is not to deny that one can distinguish methodologi-cally between the moment of recollection and discernment and the moment of carrying something out, the moment of interior solitude and the moment of communication. But this does not entail privileging the moment of seclusion over the moment of commitment. Contemplation ought itself to be active, that is, oriented toward conversion and transformation; and action ought to be contemplative, that is, enlightened, discerning, reflective. The two great sources of this incarnate spirituality, each with its respective aids, are the word of God in scripture and tradition, and the word of God in the living reality of history and in the lives of men and women filled with the Spirit.[29]

Contemplation and action, when separated from one another, cease being authentically contemplative or active.

Merton understood that to practice contemplation meant open-ing oneself to daily conversion, as I have discussed looking at our other great figures: "Contemplation is not a deepening of experience only, but a radical change in one's way of being and living."[30] This radi-cal change, to return to Pope Francis's remarks about Merton in his address, is not a change from doubt to faith, because as Merton has clearly indicated, doubt is not the enemy of faith; fear is the enemy of faith. Therefore, the major conversions that the Christian needs to undergo in her daily existence are from fear to faith and from hatred to love. Such conversion then has a measurable effect on not only an individual life, but also the life of the world: as Merton puts it, for instance, "The root of war is fear."[31] Once individual Christians carry out the ancient spiritual practices of the contemplative life, they are bound to move in a direction of nonviolence. The just peace ethic makes it clear that without ongoing spiritual development, both individually and as part of a community, we will fall short of the gospel nonviolence for which we strive.

Second, I turn to nonviolent direct action within the just peace ethic. Merton has a wary relationship here. To make this case, I return to Merton's relationship with Daniel Berrigan. Berrigan took part in the May 17, 1968, action that became known as the Catonsville Nine, in which he and eight Catholic comrades used homemade napalm to burn draft files they procured from the Selective Service office in Catonsville, Maryland.[32] Even though Berrigan revered both Merton and Day, the latter were both ambivalent about the Catonsville Nine's methodology.[33] As Merton himself wrote in response to the Catonsville Nine (which he referred to as the "Baltimore nine"), the action "frightened more than it edified" and signified that "the Peace Movement too were standing at the very edge of violence."[34] Berrigan himself was worried about what Merton thought of his taking part in this action, as he recounted in his own portrait of Merton: "He was stirred, fearful, didn't know where such acts might lead. He trusted us, but his trust was tested hard. In any case, he seemed to need more time to make up his mind."[35] Unfortunately, that time would never arrive, since Merton died only months later. Nevertheless, we do have Merton's own writings on what authentic, productive activism might look like.

One year before the Catonsville action, Merton was asked to write an article on humility. The resulting article on one of Jesus's Beatitudes, "Blessed are the meek," dealt directly with nonviolent resistance. As I noted above, citing McNeal's analysis of Merton's thought, his Gandhian side shows very clearly in these pages. Yet Merton synthesizes Gandhi's own philosophy of nonviolence with that of Jesus. The common denominator is a seeking of the truth. This is to be done at the expense of any self-aggrandizing in activism, or what Merton calls "demonic activism."[36] Many activists, Merton laments, are very concerned about the positive outcome of this or that action in which they participate. Even to a certain extent, this was on the minds of the Catonsville Nine and other such Catholic peace groups who burned draft files. The files, since they were not digitized, could not be re-created; there were also no duplicates or record of whose files had been destroyed. They were also cognizant of the media attention they would receive. Merton was less enthusiastic about such an approach, which veered from the Gandhian exclusive focus on the truth.[37]

But Merton's own interventions certainly do not disqualify non-violent direct action. These actions, though, must be enacted with the correct approach. "The tactic of nonviolence," Merton writes, "is a tac-tic of love that seeks the salvation and redemption of the opponent, not his castigation, humiliation, and defeat....[True nonviolence] is not easy in practice, especially when the adversary is aroused to a bitter and violent defense of an injustice which he believes to be just."[38] Merton's understanding of nonviolent direct action is not that it ought to consist of dramatic events such as the Catonsville Nine action (even though he may have been at least partially mistaken about their own goals), but that it should be an integral part of the Christian's daily life: "Christians have got to speak by their actions. Their political action must not be confined to the privacy of the polling booth. It must be clear and mani-fest to everybody. It must speak loudly and plainly the Christian truth, and it must be prepared to defend that truth with sacrifices, accept-ing misunderstanding, injustice, calumny, and even imprisonment or death."[39] This particular principle of the just peace ethic, therefore, fits neatly within Merton's own Christian worldview. In the United States, what Merton spells out here is countercultural, as Jim Fisher notes. But, as Mark Massa contends, it is also simultaneously cultural. Being ready to accept even death for speaking and acting boldly on behalf of our ideals, for wearing our hardest-earned feelings on our sleeves, is surely not an everyday part of American life. The just peace ethic calls for a radical reorientation of our existence in society, but it does not require sectarianism or totally isolating ourselves from that same soci-ety. Even though Merton himself entered the monastery, his was not a flight from the world; rather, it was a way to engage more intimately with it. He discovered this in something like a mystic experience in Louisville where, "at the corner of Fourth and Walnut, in the center of the shopping district, I was suddenly overwhelmed with the realization that I loved all those people." This realization is also part of his own daily conversion. Merton continues, "The whole illusion of a separate holy existence is a dream."[40]

Third, and finally, I mention Merton's understanding of relationality and reconciliation, which is another principle of the just peace ethic. One area where this was particularly necessary was in the realm of race relations in the United States. Here, two of Francis's great Americans come together seamlessly. As McNeal notes, "The influence of King on Merton cannot be overestimated."[41] As I have already noted in chapter 2, King believed that the injustices of racism and militarism were closely linked; both come together as a package, especially in the United States. To be sure, Merton believed that part of the success of the Catholic nonviolence movement would be realized only in joining with other Christian nonviolent activists, such as Martin Luther King Jr.[42] Even if Merton was particularly prophetic for a white liberal in the mid-twentieth century on the question of race, his biographer still admits, "Merton's writings on racial questions are the hardest to evaluate."[43]

Shortly before James H. Cone penned his classic volume, *Black Theology and Black Power*, Merton wrote an essay entitled "From Nonviolence to Black Power."[44] In this essay, Merton and Cone part ways to a degree on the issue of the necessity of violence. Merton seems to realize the limits of his own position: as a white man writing during that time, his perspective cannot be considered omniscient. Nevertheless, he stays strong in his support for rooting out violence: "The job of the white Christian is then partly a job of diagnosis and criticism, a prophetic task of finding and identifying the injustice which is the cause of *all* the violence, both white and black, which is also the root of war, and of the greed which keeps war going in order that some might make money out of it."[45] On the other hand, Cone claims, the Christian "must make a choice. If he decides to take the 'nonviolent' way, then he is saying that revolutionary violence is more detrimental to man in the long run than systemic violence. But if the system is evil, then revolutionary violence is both justified and necessary."[46] On the latter point of necessity, Merton and King would have disagreed with Cone. But Merton's particular openness to Black people is especially noteworthy. Merton also claimed the Christian must make a decision to support Black people: "I recognize the overwhelming justice of [their] complaint, I confess I have no right whatever to get in [their] way, and that as a Christian I owe [them] support, not in [their] ranks but in my own, among the whites who refuse to trust [them] or hear [them], and who want to destroy [them]."[47] In short, Merton wants relationality between white and Black people in society.

Therein is the starting point for reconciliation: *kenosis* and conversion. As Cone writes, "Reconciliation to God means that white people are prepared to deny themselves (whiteness), take up the cross (blackness), and follow Christ (black ghetto)."[48] How does that happen today? Even though Merton believed that the *kairos* moment had arrived for both the Black and white churches, he was unsure exactly what that would mean.[49] Merton finally concludes with this statement and following question: "The white Christian cannot…be content merely to march with his black brother at the risk of getting his head broken or of being shot. The problem is to eradicate this basic violence and unjustice from white society. Can it be done? How?"[50] The just peace ethic would claim that this actually can be done through reconciliation. If we can reconcile ourselves to God and to one another through the kenotic attitude that Cone suggests, we risk the large-scale conversion of which Merton dreamt. It would not entail only individual, dramatic moments such as the Catonsville action. Those moments would not be excluded, but they would be enfolded within a larger kairotic moment in which the Christian attitude of nonviolence, love, truth, faith, and hope overcomes all of the vices that so easily creep into our lives. From a theological perspective, this is done when white theologians teach the scholarship of people of color in their classrooms and encourage their students to think with a variety of scholars and historical figures. Pastorally, this happens when pastors of predominantly white churches begin preaching about racism from the pulpit. And yes, despite Merton's admonition, it also happens when white people join in the Black Lives Matter movement.[51]

Merton as Pontifex

One of the most infamous bridges in American history is undoubtedly the Edmund Pettus Bridge. On "Bloody Sunday," March 7, 1956, a young man named John Lewis joined the hundreds of people marching across that bridge in one of the defining moments of the Civil Rights movement in the United States. The Alabama state troopers who encountered him that day beat him mercilessly, fracturing his skull. Lewis's backpack as he crossed the bridge and took his beating was filled with books. One of them was written by Merton.[52] Some fifty years later, Lewis would call Francis's address "one of the most moving speeches I have heard in all my years in Congress." Lewis, like many of his colleagues in the chamber that auspicious day, was moved by the picture that Pope Francis painted of the United States, and in particular, his gracious words about the four great Americans. But more than that, one could only imagine that Lewis's mind wandered back to that awful day a half-century earlier when his own blood was shed for American rights. When he heard four names that were incredibly important to him, it is instructive that Merton's name was indelibly linked with a bridge in Lewis's mind. And even if that is only coincidental, it is also part of Merton's own persona in life. Even more, perhaps, in death has Merton been identified as a bridge builder, or pontifex. To conclude this chapter, I turn to this important element of Merton's legacy and identify how Pope Francis is calling American Catholics today to be bridge builders in a nation and world where our divisions often seem like impassible waters. The fourth element of Merton's life Francis identified in his address was that Merton was a "man of dialogue." I will identify and briefly examine three such impasses below that could be aided by Merton's type of dialogue.

The first of these impasses is in the Church itself. The Church in the United States, in many ways, mirrors the partisan divide between Republicans and Democrats. While time does not permit me to analyze this in great depth, it is helpful to recognize that disagreements in the Church are often among the same groups who disagree on the partisan political battlefield.[53] No one would be surprised to know that many Americans who voted for Donald Trump's reelection as president of the United States in 2020 were also outraged at Pope Francis's 2021 *motu proprio* that restricted the use of the Missal of 1962 in celebrations of the Eucharist. This shows how political differences map onto patterns of polarization in the Church.[54] Merton's own witness has the potential to build a bridge between right and left in the Church through dialogue with one another.

Even if people in the Church, as in society at large, will never be able to see eye to eye on all matters, Merton's own story of conversion is one way to see beyond the culture wars and with a view toward the future. Many of the battles between left and right in the American

84

Church have to do with questions of orthodoxy: Who is more faithful? Who is more obedient? Who is more Catholic? These questions always fail to get to the heart of the matter. As Merton was in the midst of his own conversion to Catholicism, one of his surest guides was Robert Lax (himself to convert from Judaism to Catholicism), a colleague at the college publication *Jester*.[55] During one particular moment of grace for Merton, Lax informed him that instead of wanting to be a "good Catholic," he ought to want to be a saint. Lax continued with the prerequisites for such a life: "All that is necessary to be a saint is to want to be one. Don't you believe that God will make you what He created you to be, if you will consent to let Him do it? All you have to do is desire it."[56]

This first impasse can be addressed through a renewal of catechesis on every level. On the national level, bishops must cease the practice of holding out various litmus tests over what it might mean to be a "good Catholic." This especially applies in the case of Catholic politicians.[57] Rather, the USCCB must make it possible for the Church in the United States to set itself apart, not by purity to one particular principle but by standing virtuously as Francis has called it to do. On the diocesan level, individual bishops must make it a priority to see to it that the corporal and spiritual works of mercy are being fulfilled on a daily basis. On the parochial level, pastors must preach the gospel of love with joy each and every week.[58] Each semester, I am privileged to work with a new group of young people who have just embarked on their college careers. They almost always believe that their required religious studies course is meant simply to enumerate religious rules and regulations. Almost to a person, my Catholic students have grown up in parishes that have formed them to have no interest in being saints. In truth, these parishes haven't even really been interested in forming "good Catholics." Instead, most of my students share their own experiences of being told specifically what *not* to do with their young lives. This is, as we have seen in the Church, a recipe for disaster. Not only does it cause people to leave the Church, but it betrays what ought to be most central to it: the good news of salvation. Merton's example shows us how to do better.

The second and third impasses are, quite frankly, less cumbersome than the first. This is astonishing because before the Second Vatican Council, these final two impasses were considered points of no return. They involve relations between Catholics and non-Catholics.

The second impasse to discuss here is among people of various faith traditions. Writing primarily before the breakthrough of Vatican II between the Catholic Church and other faith traditions, Merton was one of the most important figures leading to a new era of understanding between these believers. When he died in Thailand, Merton was there "to study Eastern monasticism."[59] In proclaiming such an openness to a different faith tradition, Merton was immediately latching onto the conciliar emphasis on respect and love: "We cannot truly call on God, the Father of all, if we refuse to treat in a brotherly way, any man, created as he is in the image of God" (*Nostra Aetate* 5).[60] While Merton believed especially that the East and West had much to teach each other religiously, he was especially concerned with his vocation: monasticism. He writes, "We have now reached a stage of (long-overdue) religious maturity at which it may be possible for someone to remain perfectly faithful to a Christian and Western monastic commitment, and yet to learn in depth from, say, a Buddhist or Hindu discipline and experience."[61]

Today, the realities of the twenty-first century are evident, especially among "cradle Catholics." A young person who has grown up within the Catholic community will often see no distinction between Catholicism and other religions. On the one hand, this means there is the openness necessary to have a fruitful dialogue. On the other hand, however, Merton's own example would contend that this approach is just as doomed to failure as that of the literal interpretation of the doctrine *extra Ecclesiam nulla salus* ("outside the Church no salvation"). In such a model, dialogue is impossible when at least one of the sides is insufficiently aware of their own tradition and doctrinal heritage.[62] So, in today's Church, there must be a renewed emphasis on catechetical training. On this point, I find myself in agreement with many more conservative Catholics. It is essential to know with confidence and specificity what one professes to believe if one is to join the author of the Second Letter to Timothy in truly knowing "the one in whom I have put my trust" (2 Tim 1:12). Only when Catholics know what they believe and in whom they believe can they have authentic dialogue with people of other faith traditions.

The third and final impasse for which Merton could provide a bridge is between the believer and the unbeliever. As with the traditional stalemate between Catholics and non-Catholics noted above, this relationship is much different today than it would have been before Merton's time, or even in his earlier writings. But when Merton broached this topic, the thought of Catholics conversing with atheists and agnostics about heady matters was hardly considered possible, let alone laudatory. Merton, however, sees many parallels between the contemplative life (described above) and atheism. Especially central is the concept of apophatic theology, which imagines God without images or words. Merton even makes it clear that Christianity and atheism have become one in certain areas and among certain groups, especially in the United States.[63] But insofar as it is sincere and intellectually well-considered, Merton believed that there was a future for the dialogue. "More serious," Merton contends, "is the phenomenon of a general pervasive indifference and complacency which are spread out among believers and non-believers alike."[64]

The average college classroom today is filled with many nonbelievers. I should know because these wonderful people register for my courses every semester. They arrive, sometimes convinced that there is nothing new or valuable for them to learn about God or religious traditions. Thomas Merton is a figure that provides them with solace and a sure interlocutor. Pope Francis knew this when he praised Merton during his address. Francis knew that Merton's life, which had been so interesting to the people who flocked to bookstores to buy *The Seven Storey Mountain*, had not lost its novelty even in a new century, when life was filled with new technologies. This monk, who had renounced so many material things, had not renounced the world. How could he? Even more, Francis exclaims, how can we? The dialogue for which Merton was famous and which he carried out both with members of other religions and those with no religious belief, are models for us within the Church. The first impasse, mentioned above, can take points of reference from the other two. Merton remains a model for us in the Church today. Or, as Pope Francis noted, Merton had "the capacity for dialogue and openness to God." Such an example can help those disagreeing parties within the Church to come to some agreement today.

These four great Americans are not, of course, the only exemplary figures that we see in our nation's history. Catholic and non-Catholic alike, there are so many that we are compelled to admire because of their fidelity to "a personal form."[65] This faithfulness is not a patriotism that is blind to America's faults and failings and need not even be an explicit belief in God. Francis's address calls our attention to figures who surround us every day in our quest to live up to the high calling that he has addressed to us, specifically living as part of the American culture. And so, with the example of these four great Americans in mind, I turn to a new list of figures Francis might have mentioned if he wanted to extend the examples. These nine figures are all women because most studies of American Catholicism have not focused nearly enough on them.

Chapter Five

PROPHECY FOR OUR COUNTRY AND TIME

Women in America are articulate, educated, intelligent, spiritually grounded, and wise. The church in the twentieth century was not equipped to cope with women such as we are. We were vital participants in a democratic government but silenced in the most important aspect of our lives—living the gospel values as Jesus taught us. I look forward to the church in the twenty-first century recognizing the strength and spirituality of the world. Allowing women greater participation in the teaching and governmental structure of the church would heighten the reverence members have for Mother church.

—Kathleen Padden, OSU[1]

When Pope Francis landed on American soil in 2015, he brought with him some of the best polling numbers of any public figure in the world at the time. Any political figure, including the two who would square off in the presidential race only months later, would have dreamed of such an overwhelming show of support from the people. From the very moment that Francis appeared on the loggia overlooking St. Peter's

Square some two years earlier and asked that the people gathered in the square and the millions watching around the world remember him in prayer before God, he captured many hearts. Moreover, in the days that followed, he engaged in very ordinary tasks, such as paying his own hotel bill, canceling his Argentinian newspaper subscription, and taking the bus with the cardinals who had elected him pope. On the surface, these actions don't seem like great feats, but in the Catholic imagination,[2] where symbols are always more than what they appear to be, Francis's first actions as pope have remained seared in our minds. And yet, he is a human being, and thus, imperfect. We have seen his imperfections appear on the grand stage more than once. The most egregious of these mishaps came when he accused the Chilean sexual abuse survivors of calumny in their accusations against a former prelate in that nation. After an investigation, though, Francis apologized for this misstep.

The other area where Francis has been most substantially criticized both within and outside the Church has been his understanding of the role of women in the ecclesial Body. In *Fratelli Tutti*, Francis's most recent encyclical, he chose not to cite a single woman in any of the nearly three hundred footnotes in the text. Years before promulgating this document, in his press conference en route to Rome following his 2015 pilgrimage to the United States, Francis bemoaned that "we are somewhat behind in developing a theology of women."[3] Predictably, this comment was not received well by American theologians who knew better. Merely scanning the work done by Catholic feminist theologians proved Francis's own thoughts to be off base. Obviously, Francis is not breaking any ground by failing to advance the feminist theology that has been at the core of Catholic theological study for decades now. And by only naming one woman among his four great Americans, Francis continues a long tradition of privileging male voices over female voices. To be sure, Francis has also made some strides in this area by opening more liturgical roles to women and by appointing women to important curial positions. But this is obviously insufficient.

We need not dwell on this major lacuna in Francis's vision, which also manifested itself in his 2015 address to Congress. Rather, it is more productive to present more candidates for Francis's list of great Americans. As the previous chapters of the present volume illustrate, Francis chose his four individuals for valid reasons. I do not contest those decisions. In the forthcoming pages of this chapter, however, I present three groups of American women who we could also consider great Americans. As with the previous four chapters, the next sections do not aim at biography; rather, they are theologically illustrative as to why these figures align with Francis's outlook on the United States as he expressed in his own list of selected figures. Perhaps the most obvious place to turn first is to the example of women religious.

Women Religious and the Pearl of Great Price

Among any organization's greatest treasures are the people who take the mission of that group the most seriously. In the Catholic Church, the one group that consistently stands out in this respect are women religious. Among the members of the various religious orders for women in the United States, Pope Francis could well have selected any number of people who could be categorized as great Americans. One such candidate would be Helen Prejean, CSJ.[4] One of the items that Francis has addressed with the most intensity in his pontificate has been the abolition of the death penalty. In fact, Francis noted this point explicitly during his address. There has been no greater advocate for this cause in the United States, and perhaps the world, than Prejean. Her own ministry on death row grew in fame when her first book, *Dead Man Walking*, became a major motion picture. When Susan Sarandon won the Academy Award for her performance portraying Prejean, she used her acceptance speech to thank her.

Prejean's ministry to those incarcerated on death row is supported by her writing and speaking tours around the nation, which are forms of advocacy for the abolition of the death penalty. When she speaks to audiences at Catholic parishes, universities, and high schools, she brings a message of forgiveness. Even though forgiveness is a virtue, it causes many Americans to bristle. With wars raging around the world and many Americans happy to invest in killing others, Prejean is aware that forgiveness is not simply something that happens automatically. As she writes, "Forgiveness is never going to be easy. Each day it must be prayed for and struggled for and won."[5] Why is Prejean an ideal candidate for the great American? Because she helps the scales fall from our eyes as a nation. Throughout this volume, I have frequently returned to the theme of conversion. The

United States needs a national conversion when it comes to the death penalty. Francis has reminded us of that on numerous occasions and even amended the *Catechism of the Catholic Church* to declare the inadmissibility of the death penalty. When atrocities are carried out in the search for justice, commandments are broken. When one is killed, there are often lies being told. Prejean has pointed out that basic fact: "There is an elaborate ruse going on here, a pitiful disguise. Killing is camouflaged as a medicinal act."[6]

Along with the lies we tell ourselves to justify killing a human being on death row, Prejean has made it clear repeatedly that the United States often executes innocent people. The state does this by lying throughout the investigation and the entire legal process to convince people that the perpetrator has been found despite insufficient, often even exculpatory, evidence. District attorneys often do this out of "desperation."[7] The conversions that Pope Francis has been calling Catholics to experience in their lives are from desperation to liberation, from vengeance to forgiveness. Prejean herself went through the types of conversion that Francis recommends to all of us. In her memoir, Prejean recounts a presentation she heard in June 1980 delivered by Sister Marie Augusta Neal, SNDdeN. During this presentation, Neal exclaimed of the gospel, "Integral to that good news is that the poor are to be poor no longer."[8] Prejean saw similarities between this profound moment in her own life and lives of great saints of the past, like Clare and Francis of Assisi and Teresa of Ávila.[9] The scales began falling from Prejean's eyes that very day "I don't personally know one single person or family on this earth who is poor. I'm always hanging out with middle-class or affluent *white* people like me."[10]

Prejean fits Francis's mold as a great American precisely because she has many of the same characteristics as the four he named explicitly. As Lincoln confronted a particularly barbaric practice in slavery, so Prejean faces the affront to human dignity that is the death penalty.[11] Just as King was able to connect the three evils of racism, militarism, and capitalism, so Prejean has called our attention to the fact that the death penalty victimizes the poor. As she says so often, "Capital punishment means those without the capital get the punishment."[12] Day, who herself spent time living with the poor, making their lives her own, was the model for what Prejean would do in the St. Thomas housing project.[13] And Merton's eye toward dialogue has been part of Prejean's ministry of dialogue not only with crowds, journalists, and academics, but most importantly with people on death row themselves. Prejean herself has met with Pope Francis, referring to it as the "highlight of my life."[14] On that occasion, she hand delivered a letter to Francis in which she admitted to feeling a "very deep wound at the heart of the Church, a wound which I am convinced, infects and weakens every aspect of Church life. That wound, Holy Father, is the way the Church treats women."[15] Prejean takes on the words of many women when she admits her own personal wound: "My voice is muted in my own Church, whom I love and have served all my life. It is a wound, a pain, an ache that never goes away—not only for me, but for all women."[16] Even if Pope Francis is calling for a theology of women, Prejean is reminding him that such a work is already happening, if only we have eyes to see it, and ears to hear.

Another woman religious whom Pope Francis has commended is Norma Pimentel, MJ. While her life has not hit the silver screen yet, Pimentel came into public prominence in the days leading up to Francis's 2015 pilgrimage to the United States. During an ABC broadcast of a virtual audience with Pope Francis, the pontiff singled out Pimentel for her work as the executive director of Catholic Charities of the Rio Grande Valley.[17] There is little mystery as to why Francis would be so enthusiastic about Pimentel's ministry. She works with the migrants on the southern border of the United States. Any cursory glance at Francis's pontificate clearly shows the importance he has placed on immigration. Indeed, his very first trip outside Rome was to Lampedusa, where Francis made clear his solidarity with the migrants there. In his address, Francis was clear about the importance of welcoming and caring for migrants: "When the stranger in our midst appeals to us, we must not repeat the sins and the errors of the past. We must resolve now to live as nobly and as justly as possible, as we educate new generations not to turn their back on our 'neighbors' and everything around us." Pimentel has done this with great fidelity throughout her life.

One of the most unique ways Pimentel has fulfilled her role on the border has been by breaking down ideological barriers that most Americans believe work to divide rather than unify. Pimentel, in announcing the gospel, dispels this myth: "Our job is to bring together everyone that believes and agrees that respect for human dignity is a must. I have personally witnessed the success of this philosophy in McAllen, Texas [w]here we have all joined together as one community: all faith denominations, city government, border patrol, everyone, in restoring human dignity to immigrant brothers and sisters."[18] This is important to comprehend, because it is taking place despite what Pimentel calls "extreme hatred and human suffering in our world."[19] How can we move beyond this hatred and human suffering, which seem to be a constant from one generation to the next? All members of the Church, including but not limited to the hierarchy, must be persistent in calling out offensive ad hominem partisan rhetoric that rouses people in divisive attacks on those of different races, ethnicities, sexualities, nationalities, and religions. This is the type of behavior that in no way represents Christianity. It needs to be condemned from the pulpit, in weekly parish bulletins, in CCD classes, in parochial schools, and elsewhere. But not only a negative message should be spread. The Church in the United States should boldly proclaim Francis's teaching on this subject: "An individual and a people are only fruitful and productive if they are able to develop a creative openness to others" (*Fratelli Tutti* 41).

Moreover, Francis's support of Pimentel has a larger impact, in her view: "He appreciated all that we do, especially those sisters in the United States. He was very happy to bless them for what we do and [said to] continue doing what we do and pray for him."[20] The sisters of the United States have been no strangers to dealing with investigations about their orthodoxy.[21] Francis has made clear that those days are over. Pimentel's work on the border has helped create a new life for families, which is part of the work that women religious in the United States are doing.[22] In a May 2021 video message to Pimentel, Pope Francis again thanked her for these family reunifications, noting there are four components that will help the ministry to continue to flourish. The migrants must be "welcomed, protected, accompanied, and integrated."[23] Part of being a great American in Francis's view is rising to become a great "people," which he suggests has a very particular meaning:

> A people is not the same as a country, a nation, or a state, important though these entities are. A country is a geographical entity; the nation-state is the juridical and constitutional scaffolding that gives it force....The people is always the fruit of a synthesis, of an encounter, of a fusion of disparate events that generates a whole which is greater than its parts.[24]

Once we shift our priorities to focus more on building ourselves as a people rather than only as a country, we too can become great Americans. But that requires making room for all.

Another great American who has labored to make room for all is Patricia Chappell, SNDdeN. Much like King and Day, Chappell's claim to being a great American is through uniting various issues of social injustice to highlight the clear common link among these issues. As a Black Catholic woman, however, Chappell's witness during her time as executive director of Pax Christi USA and president of the National Black Sisters' Conference is a stark reminder that the business of linking these issues under the banner of the "seamless garment" is not something that should belong only to the purview of Black Protestant men such as King or white Catholic women such as Day. Chappell's work has been in moving the Church in the United States closer to what I described at the end of chapter 2: antiracism in word and, more importantly, in deed. Part of the conversions that prophets call each person toward in their own lives is a movement out of one's "comfort zone."[25] This is precisely what Chappell has been doing in her work, and what she continues to do now as co-coordinator of the antiracism team of the Sisters of Notre Dame de Namur. The message Chappell is spreading is one that opens eyes that have long been shielded from the racist reality of the structure in which we live: "We have to move away from personal prejudice, and we have to talk about the systems that have been set up and how all of us—white, Black, brown, you name it—have been impacted by systemic racism."[26] This systemic racism, just as King claimed, goes beyond the traditional understanding of the term.

The systemic racism that is part of American culture is also wrapped up in issues of systemic violence on a national level. Chappell notes the four major tenets of Pax Christi: "Spirituality of nonviolence and peacemaking; disarmament, demilitarization and reconciliation with justice; economic and interracial justice in the United States; and human rights and global restoration."[27] Pope Francis, for his part, sees clearly that these issues are mutually intertwined. In *Fratelli Tutti*, he reflects that all of these matters continually maintain a strong presence "depending on how convenient it proves for certain, primarily economic, interests....These situations of violence, sad to say, 'have become so common as to constitute a real "third world war" fought piecemeal'" (no. 25). The idea of the "third world war fought piecemeal" is one to which Francis has returned many times in his pontificate.[28] In an American context, it should be extended to note that today a second civil war is being fought piecemeal in the form of racism and white supremacy. This is exactly the scourge that Chappell and others are trying to cut short. King had predicted it decades ago, before his death, but today, the reality of this piecemeal war is on display every time there is another incident of police brutality against a person of color. If the Church does not speak out forcefully against each and every act of police brutality, it is failing to act prophetically; it is failing its mandate.

These three examples, Prejean, Pimentel, and Chappell, are exemplary models from among the number of women religious in the United States. They are joined by countless others who fulfill Francis's criteria for a great American. But, of course, they do not hold a monopoly on this standard. Many lay women have been instrumental in bringing about revolutionary movements.

Movements and Prophecy

While it is unusual to categorize film directors as social revolutionaries, one such woman has stood out in recent years. Ava DuVernay, who directed her first film, the documentary *Compton in C Minor*, in 2007, has already established herself as one of the most prominent filmmakers of the twenty-first century. Her film *Selma* was nominated for Best Picture at the 2014 Oscars, which means that DuVernay became "the first black woman to direct a film nominated in that category."[29] After that, she "became the first Black woman to be nominated for an Academy Award in the Documentary Feature category, for directing *13th*."[30] Furthermore, in her earlier films, especially *I Will Follow* and *Middle of Nowhere*, DuVernay paid careful attention to something that has been instrumental in her later works: the inclusion of Black women. One particular aspect of DuVernay's filmmaking that stands out is her emphasis on mass incarceration in the United States, especially of the Black population.[31] This is seen especially in two of DuVernay's films: *13th* and *Middle of Nowhere*.

In *13th*, DuVernay chronicles 150 years of the way Black people have been disproportionately incarcerated. As my students watch this film each semester, I can see their faces from my position at the front of the classroom. What happens next in our predominantly white classroom is predictable. Their faces turn from horror to confusion. What DuVernay has clearly mastered is not only the collection of data and the intersplicing of different experts on the topic in an attractive way, but she has also been able to take information that is not frequently broadcast and make it plainly accessible. All of this information has the effect of shocking the viewer. DuVernay believes that *13th* "gives context" to the Black Lives Matter movement, as discussed in chapter 2. She explains this position:

> The current moment of mass criminalization, of incarceration as an industry, prison as profit, punishment as profit. And the current moment of the declaration that the lives of black people, our very breath, our very dignity, our very humanity, are valuable and matter to the world. The film is designed to get us to that point, and those three words are more than words. They are the very blood that runs within us.[32]

The very blood that runs through us is also a relational reality.

These relations come to the fore in DuVernay's film *Middle of Nowhere*, which dramatizes the other side of the mass incarceration pandemic in the United States: the loved ones who remain outside the prison walls.[33] In this book, I have tried to discuss the interrelationship of so many social injustices that the prophetic voice in American culture would address. Taking the cue of Pope Francis, we need to reexamine how the United States depends on the prison industrial complex in ways that are mostly unseen. What DuVernay and other filmmakers of conscience do is so important because they make social injustice, which often hides in plain sight, visible to the human eye through the medium of film. They are able to bring to light that which was once hidden in ways most people cannot.

Placing DuVernay in this conversation is also a reminder about the role of women in society. As one analyst notes, it is not enough simply to have Black women as lead characters in these films: "Through her characters we see that it is possible to go beyond the caricatures that typically grace the big and small screens, and we see some of the possibilities that can occur when black women control their own stories."[34] In a number of ways, then, DuVernay is able to lead us to the point of a societal conversion, which is the point of a prophet anyway. A few questions we can ask ourselves, in light of DuVernay's corpus:

97

How often are we carrying out the corporal work of mercy to visit the imprisoned? What role does prison ministry play in our local parishes? And most importantly, how are the bishops standing for prison reform, as Pope Francis has called for?

Among the most common hashtags seen today on social media is #MeToo. This movement came into popular parlance with the accusations of sexual harassment and other improprieties against some of the most recognizable men in Hollywood. However, the name Tarana Burke is unfamiliar to the vast majority of people. Burke founded the #MeToo movement years before it "went viral." She coined the phrase in 2006 and was named *Time*'s "Person of the Year" in 2017 after the many accusations of sexual harassment and assault that used that hashtag on social media. Burke has led the way to a new day for women all around the world, who, despite making up half of the world's population, only earn 1/10 the salary, own 1/100 the land, make up 3/4 of the adult illiterate, and along with their dependent children account for 2/3 of the world's starving population, and are disproportionately victims of sexual assault, rape, and human trafficking.[35] And from whom does she get her motivation? As she explained in a recent interview, "Jesus was the first activist that I knew, and the first organizer that I knew, and the first example of how to be in service to people."[36] Burke converted to Catholicism in seventh grade, but subsequently left the Church after learning of its slave-holding history.[37]

This movement has changed the way that American culture views sexual assault, and especially the way that it chooses to believe (or not believe) those survivors of these heinous actions who make the accusations in public. And yet, the movement that Burke founded still has a long way to go. We still live in a society that does not privilege the testimony of women, and even less the testimony of women of color. Moreover, Pope Francis has taken steps in this direction within the Church, especially by calling a historic summit on sexual abuse in February 2019 and promulgating the document *Vos Estis Lux Mundi* to deal with these abuses, especially among the hierarchy.

Likewise in this category of prophetic women are Sojourner Truth and Wilma Mankiller. Like the other figures covered in this book, Truth's own life is directly in line with the course being charted by Pope Francis. Truth, whose given name was Isabella Baumfree, was born a slave in New York at or around the turn of the nineteenth century. While the conversion I have been referring to in these pages has been ideological, it is worth noting Truth's experience of religious conversion. As Anne Clifford explains, "While still in her twenties she had a powerful mystical experience in which she came to really know Jesus loved her and had always loved her. Previously, she had heard of Jesus, but now she really knew him."[38] Of course, this was not just a matter of accepting this or that religious doctrine and professing it, but rather was a matter of putting it into practice in material ways. Truth modeled a type of religious experience that bore fruit in the world and influenced the way other major figures would approach the matter, in particular King. She professed even her love for white people. Imagine saying such a thing after having been a slave! This is not a throwaway line; rather, it represents a radical type of neighbor love that manifests itself especially in loving those people that are least lovable.[39]

Both an abolitionist and suffragist, Truth's most remarkable words were uttered at the 1851 Women's Convention in Akron, OH. The address, entitled "Ain't I a Woman?," was not recorded verbatim, but has been rendered in a number of different media in the many decades since its delivery. The context for this speech is important, too: Truth had risen to speak in the wake of insults and other derogatory remarks from the white men in attendance.[40] In light of this, the end of Truth's address is particularly poignant:

> I have borne thirteen children
>   and seen most sold into slavery
> and when I cried a mother's grief
>   none but Jesus heard me....
> And ain't I a woman?
>   That man in black there say
> a woman can't have as much rights as a man
>   cause Christ wasn't a woman.
> Where did your Christ come from?
>   From God and a woman!
> Man had nothing to do with him!
>   If the first woman God ever made
> was strong enough to turn the world
>   upside down, all alone,
> together women ought to be able to turn it rightside up again.[41]

Truth's virtue notwithstanding, there is also the potential for a dangerous consequence to this type of love: the structural continuation of the status quo white supremacy. We must hold ourselves responsible for complicity today.

Born in Oklahoma, and a member of the Cherokee nation, Wilma Mankiller was the first woman ever elected chief of that tribe.[42] I have already discussed that Francis's understanding of care for creation is foundational in his ethical outlook on the world. Naturally, a core tenet of that philosophy is care for the land. This is one part of Mankiller's legacy, to be certain. But Mankiller, as a member of the Cherokee nation, also believed that care for the land was sacred insofar as it connected indigenous Americans today with their ancestors.[43] This is a perfect example of what Francis calls intergenerational solidarity. He teaches, "We can no longer speak of sustainable development apart from intergenerational solidarity....Intergenerational solidarity is not optional, but rather a basic question of justice, since the world we have received also belongs to those who will follow us" (*Laudato Si'* 159). Likewise, Mankiller placed great emphasis on the ethical issues surrounding water in her own community's development and advocacy. By actually engaging in manual labor alongside her fellow Cherokees who were implementing a pipeline to deliver running water to the town of Bell, Mankiller engaged in teamwork: "According to observers, the efforts were gadugi (working together), a guiding principle in Mankiller's leadership."[44] As with the other great Americans noted in this section, Mankiller embodies much of Pope Francis's social teaching. These figures have put this teaching into practice. From where does the theory arise?

Prophets in the Academy

Being an academic myself, I am familiar with an oft-repeated critique of those in my profession: "You live in an ivory tower." The critique is sometimes warranted, I must admit. I, along with some of my colleagues, can get too fixated on the intellectual pursuits that are part of the territory in institutions of higher education. It becomes very easy to separate theory from the praxis. In this final section, I present two thinkers who have been prophets from within the academy: Elizabeth A. Johnson, CSJ,[45] and Kwok Pui-Lan. Johnson, who spent over two decades as Distinguished Professor of Theology at Fordham University in New York City, was among the first two female graduates from the doctoral program in theology at the Catholic University of America.[46] Johnson did not stop breaking new ground there, however. She has conducted some of the most important theological inquiries of the last fifty years in Catholic systematic theology. And, in fact, some of her theological motifs appear in Francis's own teachings. One term, which I introduced in chapter 3 of this volume, was *ecological conversion*, which Francis explains in paragraphs 216–21 of *Laudato Si'*. Johnson first raised the issue during her 1993 Madeleva Lecture in Spirituality at Saint Mary's College in South Bend, IN.[47] In a later text, still published before Francis ever broached the topic, Johnson writes, "In sum, ecological conversion means falling in love with the Earth as an inherently valuable, living community in which we participate, and bending every effort to be creatively faithful to its well-being, in tune with the living God who brought it into being and cherishes it with unconditional love."[48]

Prophets, as we know, often face pushback from those in power. Johnson was no different. Johnson first received pushback from the ecclesial powers-that-be in 1986, as she was applying for tenure at the Catholic University of America. The board, which includes all U.S. Catholic cardinals, had concerns over an article she had published, and staged an interrogation before granting her tenure.[49] Even though she passed this test with flying colors, she recalls the tenure process to have been a "radicalizing moment" in her life.[50] Of course, that was not to be her final run-in with the hierarchy. Like other prophets who have been constantly challenged by those who are in decision-making positions, Johnson would always prove to be a gadfly. In response to her 2007 volume *Quest for the Living God*, the USCCB Committee on Doctrine concluded that Johnson's text "does not accord with authentic Catholic teaching on essential points."[51] Johnson vigorously defended her writing by responding to each of the bishops' concerns. Finally, she explains the benefits to critical thinking in the classroom: "For students to engage with theological investigations guided by a competent professor is not only *not* harmful but can be positively beneficial, promoting intellectual and frequently spiritual growth. Students are much better prepared to face the world in flux if they have grappled with faith in this way."[52]

Instructors who have utilized Johnson's *Quest for the Living God* in the classroom will understand the perennial truths of Johnson's

101

claim in these words, and simultaneously the dangerous ground the bishops are treading when they make their claim. But what is the type of theology that instructors ought to be teaching in their classrooms? Language about God, which has been a cornerstone of Johnson's professional career, must itself be a means of conversion for those in teaching positions, whether they be bishops, professors, or parents. As Johnson writes, "The mystery of Sophia-Trinity must be confessed as critical prophecy in the midst of patriarchal rule."[53] If Pope Francis is keen to receive a theology of women, especially that which is done by women, he would do well to look first to this critical point from Johnson, and to her work in general. No authentically Catholic theology can be done today if it does not start from the knowledge that language for God has been overwhelmingly masculine over the two-millennia Christian tradition. My students often protest, "That's just the way I feel most comfortable talking about God: as a man." But as Johnson reminds us, channeling Tillich, "symbols point beyond themselves to something else, something moreover in which they participate."[54] Are we, as the Church, participating in a harmful symbol, which says that men are more like God than women? Are theologians engaging in this type of discourse in our classrooms and offices? Are we using this type of language for God in our homes, with our children who may just be learning to speak? Producing a theology of women, as Francis wishes, begins in all three of these sacred locations.

The final figure I will examine in this chapter is another person who has taken on legendary status in the academy: Kwok Pui-Lan. Kwok, who was born in Hong Kong, represents in the guild a figure who is capable of showing precisely how we can and should enter into novel relationships with Christ. We need to ask new questions about Christ if we as the Church are to flourish in the long term. No longer can we remain committed to the status quo, especially if that is not registering with people today who are yearning for a relationship with God. Kwok makes it clear that we need to see parallels between the injustices to which many feminist scholars have pointed vis-à-vis patriarchy with the injustice of colonialism. Kwok writes, "Since the 1980s, the tendency of Euro-American feminist theologians to generalise their experiences as if they speak for all women has been criticised by both white scholars and women of colour."[55] In making this claim, Kwok has not only broken new ground in Christian feminist theology in the United States, but she has also touched on a theme that Pope Francis has mentioned numerous times in his pontificate. One of the most striking messages opposed to what Francis called the "new colonialism" took place when he addressed the Second World Meeting of Popular Movements in Bolivia. Francis explained that this new colonialism is multivalent. It appears in the guises of money and of ideological oneness, which Kwok decries.[56] Francis makes it clear, however, that opposing this new colonialism is also a form of building peace in the world.[57] Peacemaking and respect for cultural differences complement one another.

Just as we must move beyond cultural limitations, Kwok argues that we must also transcend "epistemological 'limits' of our thinking about Christ."[58] Much like how Johnson raised the issue of the importance of symbol in real life for women, Kwok understands that the way scripture is interpreted has real-life effects on women who often bear the brunt of the colonizers' interpretation of a biblical text: "For many post-colonial subjects, interpretation of sacred texts is not simply an academic exercise, for action and reflection must be closely related."[59] Along these lines, Kwok makes a very important point that is worth further reflection concerning Christ: "There is no original or privileged understanding of Christ, whether at the beginning of the Christian religion or in the history of the church, that can be claimed as pure and foundational, not subject to the limitation of culture and history."[60] Part of being a great American in Francis's understanding of the term is precisely not having a monolithic understanding of the country, much less of the Christian faith. This means dreaming. Dreams of great Americans can span a wide variety of individual applications. But each of these dreams have a common destiny: the realization of justice, based on a people comprising many cultures and histories. In what follows in the final chapter, I will propose one such American dream.

Chapter Six

BECOMING GREAT AMERICANS

Following Pope Francis's blueprint for becoming a great American may look complicated. On one hand, it may take becoming the best president the country has ever seen; it could mean being the single figure most connected to the civil rights movement in the nation's history; it could mean founding a movement that cares for the poor on a daily basis; or finally, it could mean writing a bestselling book that has captivated audiences for generations and revolutionized what it means to be a spiritual writer in the Church. These figures are not average folks, even though they all came from backgrounds that would not have made them obvious choices to be named great Americans. And yet, when we read about their lives, it can be daunting to put ourselves on their level. How can we measure up to Francis's view of the great American? Nevertheless, Pope Francis calls each of us (not just Americans, but everyone) to a "bold cultural revolution" (*Laudato Si'* 114).[1] That takes a prophetic outlook, just like all of the great Americans I've examined in these pages have brought to the table. In this chapter, I examine who might be our models for great Americans in our own lives. Next, I turn to the Church: How can we follow Pope Francis's own example in the United States, which is a national ecclesial community that has been resistant to the pope's teachings in many ways? Finally, I close with a ten-step plan for how we can become great Americans in our own lives.

Finding Our Models

Naturally, there are many people after whom we can model our own lives. Each of us understands this intuitively. As youngsters, we look to our parents and grandparents, people who have had a formative impact on our lives; we want to be like them. We may think of especially influential teachers or even people from the worlds of entertainment and professional sports as worthy of emulation. As we begin our careers, there are people to whom we look for inspiration: "That's how I want to do my job someday." I will never forget, during my doctoral work, returning to Boston College for a farewell gathering honoring Father Daniel Harrington, SJ. Harrington was one of the preeminent scholars of scriptural studies in the Catholic Church, and indeed, the world. For decades, he had labored as a professor of graduate students and seminarians, authored sixty books, and written literally tens of thousands of abstracts of books and articles as the editor of *New Testament Abstracts*. In his spare time, he remained faithful to his family, his fellow Jesuits, and all Boston sports teams. At that ceremony, after he had been lauded, he rose to address those gathered, and concluded with these words: "The old saying that 'If you love what you're doing, you'll never work a day in your life,' certainly applies to me. It's all been a joy." As both a student of his and onetime editorial assistant for *New Testament Abstracts*, I witnessed that joy firsthand, and hoped to emulate it in my own career. Each person can relate to someone like this from their own vocation. Who is it that inspires you?

Moreover, there are people who joyfully give of their very selves for some greater good. Of course, this might be the job for which they are paid, but often it is something far more than this. Once again, these examples can spring to our minds very easily. I think of yet another Jesuit mentor, Father Joe Currie, SJ. One day, during a daily celebration of the Eucharist, Currie began preaching by recounting a story about that day's Responsorial Psalm. The psalm was known to all present, and indeed, to many more people than that: Psalm 23, which famously begins, "The Lord is my shepherd, I shall not want." Currie told the story of the great Shakespearean actor Richard Burton, who was visiting his home parish for the jubilee celebration for the parish's pastor, who had even taught Burton to act. The pastor implored Burton to regale the congregation by reciting the psalm. Burton complied, but only on the condition that the elderly pastor would do the same.

106

Burton nailed it! He used the ideal intonation in his voice throughout the performance, perfectly completing each verse of the psalm from memory. The congregation was thrilled. Then, the pastor rose to recite the psalm. He did so, but with great difficulty. His voice was quavering, and he may have even missed some verses in their entirety. When he sat back down, the congregation roared their approval, while wiping tears from their eyes. The old pastor was confused: Why was their reception of his performance far more jubilant than for Burton's stellar job. Burton rose and explained: "I knew the psalm, but you know the shepherd!" As Currie concluded the homily that day, I gazed around the small chapel, and others were wiping tears from their eyes. Currie, too, knew the shepherd.

I write these words in the midst of the worst pandemic to strike our world in more than a century. The COVID-19 virus has certainly changed the way we all live and will likely have such an impact far into the future. Pope Francis has pointed to the medical professionals whose lives have been marked by their selfless care for those who have fallen ill and have even died of this terrible disease. Of their sacrifice, Francis writes,

> Whether or not they were conscious of it, their choice testified to a belief: that it is better to live a shorter life serving others than a longer one resisting that call...,They are the saints next door, who have awoken something important in our hearts, making credible once more what we desire to instill by our preaching. They are the antibodies to the virus of indifference.[2]

One of the most moving days of my life was the day I was able to receive one of the vaccines that doctors and scientists labored to produce in response to this virus. But equally moving in my life, and yours I am sure, are the examples not only of these workers, but of countless human beings who give of themselves constantly so that others might not only survive but also thrive in this world. If we can think of these models, these individuals who "know the shepherd," then we have some people after whose example we can model our own lives.

What does it mean to know the shepherd? It means identifying those around us who act like Jesus, or who, in the words of Daniel Berrigan, strive to make their lives fit into the gospel. Francis, in naming four great Americans, gives us some hints as to those who might fit the bill. What is so unusual about Lincoln is that our contemporary experience of politicians is often the exact opposite of what we normally think of as a great person. We don't think of "greatness" in how many lies one can tell to get ahead, or how many donors one can woo with soaring rhetoric and empty promises. What made Lincoln exceptional is what made him great, according to Francis. Unfortunately, as I commented above, we sometimes reduce King to a single line that he uttered. And to be sure, it was a line that Pope Francis himself loves and has employed in his own writing. It is a wonderful and life-giving thing to be able to dream about the future. It is a hopeful way of existence. And yet, if it is separated from action, it is vapid. Day understood this because she was explicitly close to the poor. She did not break her life into little compartments, but rather saw her entire existence as integral. But that necessitated taking a stance. One cannot, she believed, separate the celebration of the Eucharist from feeding the hungry or protesting the war. Likewise, Merton, despite being a monk and even withdrawing to a hermitage was able to dialogue with the world. Who are the people today, in our own lives, who manifest those qualities?

When I was a sophomore in college, I participated in an immersion project in Appalachia, at a place called the Glenmary Farm. One of things we did that week was to visit a nursing home in town. It was a challenging afternoon for me. We met many people who were nearing the end of their lives, some of whom did not have the world's cheeriest dispositions. And who could blame them? The last resident we visited that day was a woman who appeared to be in her late forties. She was in her bed and as soon as she saw us, called us over to her bedside. She informed us that she had ALS and was at a point where she struggled to move her limbs; her speech was difficult to understand. Next to her bed was a very frequently used Bible. She suggested that we read her some of her favorite passages. She asked me to read Matthew 6:19–21, which is part of Jesus's Sermon on the Mount. He says, "Do not store up for yourselves treasures on earth, where moth and rust consume and where thieves break in and steal; but store up for yourselves treasures in heaven, where neither moth nor rust consumes and where thieves do not break in and steal. For where your treasure is, there your heart will be also." Then the woman nodded toward a picture hanging on the wall. She told us, "There is my treasure: my husband and daughter; they visit me a few times each day and read scripture to me. Aren't they beautiful?" That woman's name was Virginia. That exchange only lasted a few minutes, but I can't tell you what an indelible mark it made on me. Virginia, Pope Francis might say if he had met her, is a great American. We can see who these people are in our lives by noticing who their treasure is. One's greatness is almost perfectly measured by where their heart is.

A Renewed Church: Pope Francis Pointing to the Future

Since the very first days of his pontificate, Pope Francis has been constantly advocating for a "Church which is poor and for the poor."[3] When most of us think of the Church, though, poverty is not the first thing that comes to mind. Nevertheless, I would argue with some liberation theologians that what Francis proposes is only the first step to the place where the Church can become its most authentic self. As Jon Sobrino argues,

> The Church of the poor is not a Church for the poor but a Church that must be formed on the basis of the poor and that must find in them the principle of its structure, organization, and mission. For the same reason I maintain that this Church does not conceive of the poor as "part" of itself, even a privileged part, but thinks of them rather as the "center" of the whole.[4]

How often do we think the United States is the center of the whole Church? Or do we continue to push people to the margins? Gregory Boyle puts it this way:

> Soon we imagine, with God, this circle of compassion. Then we imagine no one standing outside of that circle, moving ourselves closer to the margins so that the margins themselves will be erased. We stand there with those whose dignity has been denied. We locate ourselves with the poor and the powerless and the voiceless. At the edges, we join the easily despised and the readily left out. We stand with the demonized so that the demonizing will stop. We situate

ourselves right next to the disposable so that the day will come when we stop throwing people away.[5]

In what places is the Church in the United States doing these things? To be sure, it is happening, and many of you reading these words may be crucial to your local parish's efforts on this front. You may be in daily solidarity with the poor of your town, or even of other nations in the world. In Francis's dream, you may be part of the solution that means bringing together everyone as one people. But it seems as though this dream is marginalized in our Church. Too frequently, the Church seems closer to the rich and powerful than to the poor. As part of the very same pastoral visit during which Francis addressed Congress, he also visited New York, where he led Vespers for the priests and religious of the city at St. Patrick's Cathedral. But sitting in the front pews were some of the archdiocese's wealthiest donors. Why?

The answer to that question ought to make every Catholic in the United States uneasy. Their wealth got them into that building that day. Nevertheless, there is always reason to hope that the Church in the United States can grasp Francis's own call toward holiness. In an essay published in 1977, Ignacio Ellacuría noted that the "conception of the church as church of the poor has great practical consequences."[6] In that essay, Ellacuría notes four. Here, I follow Ellacuría's argument and draw out what these practical consequences might mean, specifically in the United States, and how they might urge American Catholics toward the conversion experiences necessary to become prophetic great Americans.

The first of these practical consequences, Ellacuría contends, is *the Christian faith must mean something real and palpable in the life of the poor.*[7] When the Church deepens its concern for the poor, do they remain poor or do they acquire what they need to flourish as human beings? Do they come to have enough money to have a permanent residence, food to eat, and basic necessities? Ellacuría reminds us of what salvation consists:

> The preference of Jesus for the poor is not a purely affective preference; it is also a real dedication to their achievement of a salvation that is not only a promise of a life beyond earth but is eternal life already present. It is impossible to ignore

all the real and historical work that Jesus did for the poor of his time.[8]

If the Church is content to say that we are "helping" the poor because we simply want to avoid eternal damnation, that may be an acceptable place to start, but its focus is pointing inward rather than outward. The Church will never arrive at the location to which Sobrino, Ellacuría, or Boyle refer if it is a matter of top-down assistance or aid to those most in need. This does not account for solidarity. Ellacuría wrote from a much different social location than the United States. Writing from El Salvador, one of the world's poorest nations, Ellacuría was still able to see clearly that the ruling class possessed a particular amount of wealth that could greatly impact the lives of the poorest. How much more is such an outcome possible in the United States? Francis was clear on such a point, noting that these inequalities have an illogical outcome:

> The foreign debt of poor countries has become a way of controlling them, yet this is not the case where ecological debt is concerned. In different ways, developing countries, where the most important reserves of the biosphere are found, continue to fuel the development of richer countries at the cost of their own present and future. (*Laudato Si'* 52)

Once again, the injustices that arise from severe discrepancies in wealth have adverse effects on many areas of a nation's common life. The United States, being such a rich nation, has a special responsibility to pay off its debt to poorer nations.

The second practical consequence Ellacuría enumerates is that "the Christian faith, far from being an opiate—and not only a social opiate—should establish itself as what it is: a principle of liberation."[9] What is an opiate today in the United States? Was Marx right in describing religion in such a way? In one sense, I feel compelled to answer in the affirmative. Too many American Catholics believe in a religious system whereby what we are working toward is something that will be rewarded, or not, in the life to come.[10] Therefore, a significant number of American Catholics believe that any sufferings that human beings experience today will only be temporary, and religion is there to dull those sufferings until such a time when they will disappear. Ellacuría is clear that such a viewpoint not only is wrong, but it infects the

111

social fabric of a people. Rather than present a narcotized existence, the Christian faith ought to place itself in socially precarious positions when there is injustice. He writes these provocative words: "While not all persecution is a sign and miracle proving the authenticity of faith, the absence of persecution by those who hold power in a situation of injustice is a sign, irrefutable in the long range, that the proclamation of its message lacks evangelical courage."[11] But the Church is also not simply a "sociopolitical force" either, which means that it must recall the origin of its work: the Jesus of the Gospels.[12] All too often in the United States, as I have written in earlier chapters of this volume, the U.S. bishops seem to be reducing their charge to a partisan position. This is part of the reason they have lost so much credibility in recent decades. Ellacuría is not arguing that bishops ought not make political statements; far from it. On the contrary, almost every statement a bishop utters will be political because of its focus: the *polis*. But the source of these statements must be Jesus Christ, who himself identified with the poor in his own life and death. To take the essential differentiation proffered by Gustavo Gutiérrez, "Material poverty is a scandalous condition. Spiritual poverty is an attitude of openness to God and spiritual childhood."[13] But this does not explain why Jesus would become poor to the point of death. Gutiérrez goes on: "But he does not take on the human sinful condition and its consequences to idealize it. It is rather because of love for and solidarity with others who suffer in it."[14] Can the Church practice this solidarity with faithfulness today?

This question brings us to Ellacuría's third practical consequence of the Church of the poor: "The church of the poor does not permit us to make a sharp separation between faith and religion, at least in specific social contexts and in the early stages of a conscientizing process."[15] In the United States today, do many people see a difference between faith and religion? Or, if they do, is it even relevant at all? Ellacuría is careful here not to make a theological blunder on this point. He understands that there is a difference between these two terms, and yet he also realizes that in certain contexts, the difference can be fatal. In the Salvadoran context in which he was writing, Ellacuría notes, "On the one hand, the distinction can turn faith into something purely individual and purely parochial and not structural; or on the other, it can bypass the need to embody the faith 'also' in religious form, as the 'corporeal' nature that the social reality requires."[16] Anyone who has been to a Catholic liturgy has been surrounded by people who fall into the problems that Ellacuría describes here. Even though the United States today is in both a different culture and a different time than the one from which Ellacuría wrote, we see the type of polarizations he describes.

Ellacuría especially warns against those clerics who become partisan figures: "It is wrong when priests collectively abandon or undervalue the proclamation and living practice of the sources of faith in order to engage in political struggle. To claim that this is 'faith' over against 'religion' involves a secularization of the faith that goes beyond the need to historicize and politicize it."[17] During the 2020 U.S. presidential election, anyone interested could access dozens of new videos each week from American Catholic priests opining about the election. In theory, such sermonizing[18] could be helpful if it mentioned particular issues to consider when casting one's ballot. Instead, these videos showed priests demonizing Joseph Biden from the pulpit, usually for upholding abortion rights, but sometimes for other issues too. The worst offender was Father Frank Pavone, who is president of Priests for Life and has been stripped of his priestly faculties by his bishop in Amarillo, Texas. Pavone would frequently speak wearing Donald Trump merchandise and served for a time as one of Trump's advisors.[19] Ellacuría is clear: "Evangelization can and must be political and historical, but, above all, it is the proclamation of the salvation that is offered and given to us in Jesus."[20] The actions on display from Pavone and other priests like him, often preaching during televised Masses on EWTN, was anything but this form of evangelization. More often, it was idolatry.

The fourth and final practical consequence that Ellacuría lists is that *"this church of the poor must not become another form of elitism."*[21] Here, Boyle's sentiment above brings us back to the point of these practical consequences. If there is no elitism, there are also no margins. Both elitism and margins are erased in one action of caring for all. As an example, Ellacuría turns to Salvadoran father Rutilio Grande, who had been murdered shortly before Ellacuría's writing, and cites at length the reflections of the peasants with whom Grande had been exceptionally close in his ministry. Of Grande, Ellacuría writes, "He related to the humble people to show them that the gospel must be lived in struggle, not to leave it in the air, but to be able to overcome injustice, exploitation, and misery. That is why the enemies of the people decided to kill him along with his people."[22] Over and again, Jesus shows himself to be close to each individual with whom he interacted in the Gospels. Is this our experience in the Church today, especially in our parishes in the United States? Are bishops, priests, deacons, lay ministers coming close to the people with tenderness and compassion? If not, why? If so, then why are so many people leaving the Church? Many see elitism at play, and this can manifest itself in many ways. Obviously, the fancy vestments can put people off. The titles and places of honor are not the type of outward display of equality that people want to see from Church leaders. There must be a shift in the ecclesial atmosphere if the American Church is to take Francis's vision to heart. Or as Jon Sobrino summarizes it, "When the poor are at the center of the Church, they give direction and meaning to everything that legitimately...and necessarily...constitutes the concrete Church: its preaching and activity, its administration, its cultural, dogmatic, theological, and other structures."[23] With this guidance in mind, I conclude by introducing ten ways in which we can fulfill Francis's own dream for us.

Ten Steps to Becoming Great Americans

What follows on this list requires very hard work, communal outreach, and the whole Body of Christ working together toward a common goal. In the following ten suggestions, I conclude my reflections where I have tried to argue that if we want to be great Americans according to Pope Francis's blueprint, we must first be willing to lose our lives. Greatness in the eyes of the world, after all, is much different than what Jesus calls his disciples to in the Gospels.[24] In the United States, greatness is readily found in the hopes and dreams of many of my college students. They, like many Americans, really want to land a great job, earn a lot of money, buy a mansion, a few cars, and retire at an early age with plenty of opportunity for vacation time. One passage from scripture often stops them in their tracks; it is one of my favorite things to teach all semester long. The passage is reasonably simple and yet endlessly profound. In the middle of the first century, St. Paul wrote these stunning words to the Corinthians. Like many of my students and me, the first readers of this message some two millennia ago would have been struck by the challenge of Paul's words: "If for this life only we have hoped in Christ, we are of all people most to be pitied"

(1 Cor 15:19). How can we take this passage to heart as Christians who also happen to be American? I suggest these ten steps, as inspired by Pope Francis's Address to Congress.[25] I supplement them with some concrete ideas that might help us to add these steps as part of our daily routines.

1. *Satisfy common needs by stimulating the growth of all society's members, especially those in situations of greater vulnerability or risk.* We are only as strong as our weakest members. As soon as we realize the truth behind this statement, we will begin heading toward the type of success that Pope Francis is suggesting for us as a people. So, necessarily, we have to ask ourselves, "Who is most vulnerable in our society right now?" As soon as we identify these people, we can set out to make their lives part of our own. There will always be vulnerable and weak people whom we can help. In the case of vaccination, it is up to each responsible adult to be a great American by contacting local and state elected officials to make it clear that safety is of the utmost importance and ought to be protected. But in each of our lives, at every turn, there is someone who does not have a voice. How can we speak on their behalf?

2. *Build a better life for families.* When Pope Francis made this point in his address, he was talking especially about parents who wanted to make life better for their families, but we can extend this point even further. Society should make it possible for families to have a more comfortable existence. A few years after the pope's address, pictures and video footage of children packed into cages on the Mexico-U.S. border began emerging and making the rounds on various media platforms. This led to protests all across the country to let the kids out of the cages. The reality is that every parent who viewed those pictures should have been able to picture their own children there. Or, conversely, every child who saw their contemporaries might have imagined what it would be like to be in these cages without their mothers and fathers. This is not only a nightmare, but a sin that cries out to

heaven. Much of the political discourse that surrounded those days offered the logic that by securing the southern border of the United States, we were making the country safer. But safer from whom? As Francis remarked in his address, and has throughout his pontificate, countries with resources such as the United States are obliged to welcome migrants. Who was being protected, who was safer, because those children were locked away? Being great Americans means not only providing for our own families, but for all families. Until that happens, we cannot become a great people. But we see figures, like Sister Norma Pimentel, leading the way. If we follow, we are reaching our potential.

3. *Enter into dialogue with the many elderly persons who are a storehouse of wisdom forged by experience and with all those young people who are working to realize their great and noble aspirations.* When I heard Pope Francis make this plea during his address, I was immensely grateful for two reasons. First, I had known and loved my grandparents, and even some of my great-grandparents. Living with and learning from them has been one of the greatest gifts of my life. Raconteurs extraordinaire, they were extravagant in the love that they poured out on their family. As they aged, I witnessed, like many of you have with your own parents and grandparents, how they physically and mentally slowed in ways that I couldn't have imagined. And yet, in those times, I learned some of life's greatest lessons from them. One of them was to savor every minute you get to spend with people you love. Likewise, I was drawn to these words from Francis because seated around me in the student center were my own students, who were attending a campus ministry-sponsored viewing party to watch the address. Later that day, I went to teach and talked about what we had witnessed earlier. Spending time with young people, whose lives are entirely ahead of them, is an immense privilege. The young and the old merge because they share a common humanity and the realization that we all have something to learn and something to teach, regardless of our state in life.

4. *We must be a people of hope and healing, of peace and justice.* The context for this statement from Francis was a discussion of the aforementioned reality in our world that so many people are unable to see any alternative except good and evil; for many, there is no gray area. Sadly, yet predictably, this set of beliefs leads to tremendous polarization in the United States. The presidential elections of 2016 and 2020 represented a particularly venomous breakdown in dialogue among the various political factions in the country, culminating in the insurrection at the U.S. Capitol building on January 6, 2021. The Church has a unique role to play in response to these tumultuous times. Instead of being a source of division, bishops and priests need to begin preaching and teaching an ethic of healing. This would mark a substantial change from the rhetoric on display during both of those election seasons. It would also necessitate a recognition that Catholics, too, are as polarized as the secular society is. One possible response would be for each respective enclave of the Church to hear preaching from the pulpit that is out of the ordinary. As Michael Peppard has observed, "Although Catholics do always encounter Jesus during the Liturgy of the Eucharist, if the moral perspectives of parishioners are never challenged during the Liturgy of the Word, the fullness of Jesus' message is not being manifested."[26] When Church expands its horizons and refuses to be placed within an ideological box, we will enjoy a much-needed balm for American culture. As Robert Schreiter argued, the Church is in a privileged position to tackle these issues with three unique resources: "The first is its message about reconciliation and the spirituality that flows out of it. The second is the power of its rituals. And the third is its capacity to create communities of reconciliation."[27]

5. *Politics is an expression of our compelling need to live as one, in order to build as one the greatest common good: that of a community that sacrifices particular interests in order to share, in justice and peace, its goods, its interests, its social life.* How frequently are we looking to share

what we have with others? As I mentioned earlier, St. Ignatius Loyola considers that particular trait essential if one wants to love like God. Political love, as I noted in chapter 1, can lead to the fostering of a great American people. But I suggest that the Church ought to take the first step down this road by claiming that politics as we know it is broken. By saying this, I do not mean to say that John Courtney Murray's understanding of Catholicism's relationship with the American experiment was entirely mistaken. Rather, the Church needs to ask itself constantly what the gospel demands of us as a people. Pope Francis reminds us of the imperative behind this change of pace in society: "We need to strengthen the conviction that we are one single human family. There are no frontiers or barriers, political or social, behind which we can hide, still less is there room for the globalization of indifference" (*Laudato Si'* 52). As the term implies, the globalization of indifference has infected the entire world. Here in the United States, the problem is especially acute. Who cares if people in other countries are suffering? Who cares if babies are being aborted? Who cares if migrants are dying as they try to cross into our country? Who cares? Francis is saying that if we wish to become a great people, we must care. It is the only Christian way. This means redoubling our efforts on a parochial and diocesan level to be in solidarity with all of these people who are suffering injustices.

6. *If we want security, let us give security; if we want life, let us give life; if we want opportunities, let us provide opportunities.* A major component of Catholic social teaching is participation. When Francis is discussing opportunities that might arise, we have to ask ourselves the simple question: "Who has no opportunities in our country?" Once we produce an answer to this question, we quickly see who is not allowed to participate in the workings of society. Catholic social teaching is clear: "The person is called to participate in shaping society in such a way as to promote the well-being of its members, and it is in this act of participation that the essential dignity of the person

is both achieved and revealed."[28] The Church is able to model participation in society on a very basic level. Is every member of the Church allowed to participate in structural decisions at the local and diocesan levels, let alone the national or universal levels? Diocesan bishops and parish pastors need to ask themselves whether they are promoting the human dignity of their congregants. Only once that has been accomplished can they adequately preach on the issue. And preach they must. They ought to be especially cognizant of any legislation that is being advanced that would limit in any way the right to vote in elections. This type of legislation is racist, a holdover from Jim Crow-era laws. Until the Church stands for voting rights for all, they are not promoting participation, and are, therefore, denying human dignity.

7. *The fight against poverty and hunger must be fought constantly on many fronts, especially its causes.* When Pope Francis is calling us to focus on this issue, he is asking us to look beyond what the Church is already doing. By any account, the Church sponsors all types of soup kitchens and other services in which meals can be shared with poor people and families in need. But the goal is to arrive at a day when those people will no longer need these services. So, when Pope Francis calls us to fight the "causes" of poverty and hunger, he is saying that the Church should act on behalf of everyone in society. Why do people go hungry? It is clear that Francis already is aware of the main source of the problem: greed and individualism. And his words for ecclesial communities that ignore the structural root of these issues are harsh:

> Any Church community, if it thinks it can comfortably go its own way without creative concern and effective cooperation in helping the poor to live with dignity and reaching out to everyone, will also risk breaking down, however much it may talk about social issues or criticize governments. It will easily drift into a spiritual worldliness camouflaged by religious practices,

unproductive meetings and empty talk. (*Evangelii Gaudium* 207)[29]

All too often, these types of communities are obvious to anyone with eyes to see. And yet, other parish communities integrate themselves into the lives of the poor and work to make sure they understand they belong in the community. This is the type of witness for which Francis is calling.

8. *Being at the service of dialogue and peace also means being truly determined to minimize and, in the long term, to end the many armed conflicts throughout our world.* This practical step is one of the most important we can take away from Francis's address to Congress. The fact is that in that address, he cited three Christians who were absolutely committed to gospel nonviolence.[30] When the final report is written on Francis's pontificate when it comes to issues of war and peace, there will be a very important development of doctrine to review. Just as with the emendation to the *Catechism* on the matter of the death penalty, and just as *Amoris Laetitia* has advanced the conversation on reception of holy communion for some divorced and civilly remarried persons, Francis has made clear that war and peace is not a settled question in Catholic morality. As he writes in *Fratelli Tutti*, "We can no longer think of war as a solution, because its risks will probably always be greater than its supposed benefits. In view of this, it is very difficult nowadays to invoke the rational criteria elaborated in earlier centuries to speak of the possibility of a 'just war.' Never again war!" (no. 258). In saying these words, Francis followed in the path trod by his predecessors since Pope John XXIII. However, Francis set the foundation in place for even new inroads to be made on this issue with the corresponding footnote to the previous passage. This note reads, "Saint Augustine, who forged a concept of 'just war' that we no longer uphold in our own day, also said that 'it is a higher glory still to sway war itself with a word, than to slay men with the sword, and to procure or maintain peace by peace,

120

not by war'" (no. 258, n. 242). Never before had a pope stated that we no longer uphold the Augustinian just war doctrine. The Church has amended it, but it has never abrogated it. This is a monumental plea to the people of the world to work for peace in ways that we have not accomplished.

9. *Dream big.* I have returned to this theme throughout the book, but it is worth revisiting here as the penultimate concrete idea because it is so central to Francis's message. The objection is obvious: there are few things as ephemeral as dreams. However, as Francis has indicated, and as I showed in discussing the life of Martin Luther King Jr., dreams need not be distracting thoughts that get in the way of the busy-ness of our everyday lives. Far from it! Rather, dreams ought to compel us to action. In his reflections on how people of the world ought to be reacting to the COVID pandemic, Francis warns that if things simply return to normal after a crisis, then we have wasted our time. Rather, Francis writes, "This is a moment to dream big, to rethink our priorities—what we value, what we want, what we seek—and to commit to act in our daily life on what we have dreamed of. What I hear at this moment is similar to what Isaiah hears God saying through him. Come, let us talk this over. Let us dare to dream."[31] By using the word *dare* in that last sentence, Francis reminds us that dreaming is not a passive activity. Much like the last concrete step, it is active.

10. *Pray.* Finally, to become great Americans, we must pray. It is possible that Francis is the single most understanding pope in the entire history of the Church when it comes to interacting with non-Catholics, and even atheists. At many of his gatherings, he has elected not to offer a blessing with the traditional formula, for fear of causing any discomfort in nonbelievers in the crowd. Likewise, Francis does not mean to force prayer on people who do not pray. At the conclusion of his book of conversations with Austen Ivereigh, he urges the reader, "When you feel the twitch, stop and pray. Read the Gospel, if you're a Christian. Or just create space inside yourself to listen.

Open yourself...decenter...transcend."[32] But Francis was convinced, in naming who he did as great Americans, that prayer was at the very heart of their life, even in the case of Lincoln, who was not especially religious. But for what shall we pray? We should continue offering prayer to God for all the people and things that we already keep in mind during this sacred time: our families, friends, and general health. We should offer thanksgiving for blessings, and supplication for our desires; we should cry out in lament for the injustices that bring the world to its knees. We ought to bring together prayers that don't often get connected: an end to war, abortion, and the death penalty. We should pray for equal treatment of women in the Church as well as secular society. We should recall the LGBTQ+ community that is marginalized throughout the world and within their own ecclesial communion. Being great Americans means standing at our national borders with arms open to those who are in desperate need. Perhaps most of all, being great Americans will require, here and now, prophesying against white supremacy in all its ugly manifestations. That sin, as so many great Americans have shown, is intimately connected to all the other social sins we can think of.

How shall we pray? First, we should pray liturgically. As the Fathers of Vatican II rightly teach, "The liturgy is the summit toward which the activity of the Church is directed; at the same time it is the font from which all her power flows" (*Sacrosanctum Concilium* 10).[33] Clearly, the Eucharist is at the very center of the Church's liturgical prayer, but as we move further into the twenty-first century, and in light of the COVID pandemic, being great Americans from within the Church will mean expanding what we recognize as liturgy. This will require wider practice of the Liturgy of the Hours, and other extraeucharistic liturgies, which can be led by laypeople, and especially laywomen. Teaching prayer to young people is of the highest importance in the life of the Church. So many people believe that a rudimentary education in the faith is sufficient. But Dean Brackley disagrees, wisely observing, "We should fear for the future if students are graduating with first-class training in, say, economics and only a first-Communion or a *Newsweek* understanding of the faith. Even more, keeping faith requires orthopraxis, including conspicuous respect for the rights of workers and all vulnerable members of the learning community."[34] Notice the connection Brackley makes there. There is no faith, there is no prayer, unless it gets us to the streets.[35] Pope Francis puts it this way: first we pray, "and then act. Call up, go visit, offer your service. Say you don't have a clue what to do, but maybe you can help. Say you'd like to be part of a different world, and you thought this might be a good place to start."[36] This is precisely what Brackley did after his Jesuit brethren and their lay associates were massacred in 1989. Showing up is part of the fight for justice. At each Eucharist I attend, as the priest raises the chalice before receiving communion, I continue the practice I observed hundreds of times from Father Joseph Currie, SJ. At that same point in the eucharistic celebration, he would pronounce the words of Psalm 116: "What return shall I make to the Lord for all the good things God has done for me? I will take the cup of salvation and call on the name of the Lord." For a Christian looking to become a great American, that is more than a prayer of thanksgiving; it is an oblation. In uttering those profound words and receiving the bread of life and cup of eternal salvation, the Church moves forward into the world. In so doing, our very lives become prayers. And may the Church say, Amen!

NOTES

Preface

1. See Gerard O'Connell, *The Election of Pope Francis: An Inside Account of the Conclave That Changed History* (Maryknoll, NY: Orbis Books, 2019), 3–15.

2. See John L. Allen Jr., *The Rise of Benedict XVI: The Inside Story of How the Pope Was Elected and Where He Will Take the Catholic Church* (New York: Doubleday, 2005), 114.

3. Allen, *The Rise of Benedict XVI*, 114.

4. Pope Francis, "Audience to Representatives of the Communications Media" (March 16, 2013), http://www.vatican.va/holy_father/francesco/speeches/2013/march/documents/papa-francesco_20130316_rappresentanti-media_en.html.

5. For a sampling of the most obvious examples, see the Vatican's archive of Francis's writings, homilies, and speeches, http://www.vatican.va/content/francesco/en.html. On poverty, see *Evangelii Gaudium* 186–216; on peace, see *Evangelii Gaudium* 217–37 and *Fratelli Tutti.* 256–62; on creation, see *Laudato Si'*.

6. By this, I mean to say that Francis has bypassed the normal guidelines for selecting bishops in choosing the metropolitan archbishops of the following archdioceses: Chicago (Blase Cupich), Newark (Joseph Tobin), and Washington, DC (Wilton Gregory). Francis has also named these three men to serve in the College of Cardinals.

7. Stephen J. Fichter, Thomas P. Gaunt, Catherine Hoegeman, and Paul M. Perl, *Catholic Bishops in the United States: Church*

Leadership in the Third Millennium (New York: Oxford University Press, 2019), 28. When the authors claim that Francis is interested in bishops having a "pastoral orientation," they are pointing to the fact that Francis has appointed more bishops who had spent greater periods of time as pastors rather than administrators in their priestly careers. This is in contradistinction to Popes John Paul II and Benedict XVI. Fifty-eight percent of the bishops appointed by Francis consider themselves "traditional," compared to only 42 percent of those appointed by Benedict XVI, and 39 percent appointed by John Paul II (29).

8. John Gehring, *The Francis Effect: A Radical Pope's Challenge to the American Catholic Church* (Lanham, MD: Rowman and Littlefield, 2015), 147.

9. However, it ought to be stated very clearly that many figures who fit more neatly in the category of culture warrior often consider their own rhetoric to be prophetic. For example, see the comments of Bishop Daniel Jenky, CSC, comparing President Barack Obama to Adolf Hitler and Joseph Stalin in 2015, accessed May 18, 2022, https://www.youtube.com/watch?v=YJOnVLSFyE8. Archbishop William Lori defended these statements by illustrating it as prophetic speech: "Sometimes prophets are thought to be unduly alarmist, and sometimes their speech is a little bit strong. But that's what prophetic speech always has been." See Barbara Bradley Hagerty, "Bishops Launch 2-Week Campaign against Health Law," *NPR*, June 20, 2012, https://www.npr.org/2012/06/20/155421644/bishops-launch-2-week-campaign-against-health-law.

10. Pope Francis, "Meeting with the Bishops of the United States" (September 23, 2015), http://www.vatican.va/content/francesco/en/speeches/2015/september/documents/papa-francesco_20150923_usa-vescovi.html.

11. "Homily of Pope Francis," 2013 Chrism Mass (March 28, 2013), http://www.vatican.va/content/francesco/en/homilies/2013/documents/papa-francesco_20130328_messa-crismale.html.

12. I say this is timeless, but as these words are printed, Joseph Biden is serving as the president of the United States, and in so doing is only the second Roman Catholic ever to hold that position. Therefore, the question is also timely.

Introduction

1. Lawrence Boadt, *Reading the Old Testament: An Introduction* (New York: Paulist Press, 1984), 306.

2. Nancy C. Ring et al., *Introduction to the Study of Religion*, 2nd ed. (Maryknoll, NY: Orbis Books, 2012), 199.

3. Richard J. Clifford, "The Berrigans: Prophetic?" in *The Berrigans*, ed. William VanEtten Casey and Philip Nobile (New York: Avon Books, 1971), 31.

4. Clifford, "The Berrigans: Prophetic?," 32.

5. Margaret Farley, "Prophetic Discourse in a Time of AIDS," in *Changing the Questions: Explorations in Christian Ethics* (Maryknoll, NY: Orbis Books, 2015), 241.

6. David L. Petersen, *The Prophetic Literature: An Introduction* (Louisville, KY: Westminster John Knox, 2002), 1.

7. Petersen, *The Prophetic Literature*, 5.

8. Joseph Blenkinsopp, *A History of Prophecy in Israel* (Philadelphia: Westminster Press, 1983), 19–20.

9. Gerhard von Rad, *The Message of the Prophets* (New York: Harper and Row, 1967), 9.

10. von Rad, *The Message of the Prophets*, 9–10.

11. All Bible translations are from the NRSV.

12. Daniel Berrigan, *Isaiah: Spirit of Courage, Gift of Tears* (Minneapolis: Fortress Press, 1996), 29–30.

13. At the outset, I should say that I will be referring to all the Minor Prophets collectively as the "Book of the Twelve." As David Petersen explains, "The Book of the Twelve contains some of the earliest as well as latest exemplars of prophetic literature. At one end of the spectrum, Amos reflects conditions of the mid-eighth century. On the other hand, Zechariah 9–14 dates from well into the Persian period (ca. 550–330). The Twelve thus covers a period of roughly four hundred years, including the period of two kingdoms, exile, and restoration." None of the major prophets—including the 240-year sweep of the three Isaiahs—can compare with the breadth of the Book of the Twelve (170–71).

14. Amos is working off of a prophetic tradition that was already three or four hundred years old. He is not the first prophet, but rather

the earliest prophet on this list of fifteen that have books of the Bible named after them.

15. Gene M. Tucker and J. Andrew Dearman, "Amos," in *The Harper Collins Study Bible (NRSV)*, rev. ed. (San Francisco: Harper Collins, 2006), 1216.

16. J. David Pleins, *The Social Visions of the Hebrew Bible*: A *Theological Introduction* (Louisville, KY: Westminster John Knox, 2001), 369.

17. Pleins, *Social Visions of the Hebrew Bible*, 375. In order to see how this has impacted the United States, one need only look to the election of Donald Trump as president.

18. Pleins, *Social Visions of the Hebrew Bible*, 376. Even the most radical of the "great Americans" to whom Francis refers—Dorothy Day—does not necessarily recommend overthrowing the state, but rather a deep reform of the state's current practices.

19. Petersen, *Prophetic Literature*, 191.

20. von Rad, *Message of the Prophets*, 255.

21. Throughout the present volume, I will emphasize that a strong commitment to nonviolence is present in three of the four Americans Francis commends to our attention in his address: Day, King, and Merton.

22. This passage, though more frequently cited from Isaiah's prophecy, is the justification for the Plowshares movement, which began in 1980 as a means of committed groups trying to disarm nuclear weapons in the United States and throughout the world. For more on this phenomenon, see Sharon Erickson Nepstad, *Religion and War Resistance in the Plowshares Movement* (Cambridge: Cambridge University Press, 2008).

23. On this point, I am indebted to the work of the late G. Simon Harak, SJ (himself a prophet), who constantly reminded listeners of this point in many public lectures.

24. Gerhard Lohfink, *Jesus of Nazareth: What He Wanted, Who He Was* (Collegeville, MN: Michael Glazier, 2012), 185.

25. Walter Brueggemann, *The Prophetic Imagination* (Philadelphia: Fortress Press, 1978), 11.

26. "The Church Serves Personal, Communal, and Transcendent Liberation," March 23, 1980, The Archbishop Romero Trust, http://www.romerotrust.org.uk/homilies-and-writings/homilies/church -serves-personal-communal-and-transcendent-liberation.

27. Romero was also critical of United States foreign policy with regard to El Salvador. See his letter to President Jimmy Carter of February 17, 1980, in *Voice for the Voiceless: The Four Pastoral Letters and Other Statements* (Maryknoll, NY: Orbis Books, 1985), 188–90.

28. Daniel Berrigan, "You Vested Us This Morning," *America* 70, no. 3 (October 23, 1943): 75.

29. See Shawn Francis Peters, *The Catonsville Nine: A Story of Faith and Resistance in the Vietnam Era* (New York: Oxford University Press, 2012).

30. Even though Berrigan was ostracized by his Jesuit confreres, he was very close friends with two of the principal figures in this text: Day and Merton.

Chapter One: Abraham Lincoln and Freedom

1. Frederick Douglass, "Lincoln and the Colored Troops," in *Reminiscences of Abraham Lincoln,* ed. Allen Thorndike Rice (New York: Harper and Brothers, 1909), 323. As the historian Doris Kearns Goodwin notes, "This remark takes on additional meaning when one realizes that Douglass had met dozens of celebrated abolitionists, including Wendell Phillips, William Lloyd Garrison, and Salmon Chase. Apparently, Douglass never felt with any of them, as he did with Lincoln, an 'entire freedom from popular prejudice against the colored race.'" See Goodwin's *Team of Rivals: The Political Genius of Abraham Lincoln* (New York: Simon and Schuster, 2005), 207–8.

2. Even though Lincoln was not active in any faith community, it is worth noting that he used the Bible throughout his public career. In his many political speeches, Scripture was one of his most oft-cited sources, along with Shakespeare. On this point, see Elton Trueblood, *Abraham Lincoln: Theologian of American Anguish* (New York: Harper & Row, 1973), 48–71.

3. For the best single volume of these documents, along with other documents from the Synod of Bishops, and national episcopal conference, see David J. O'Brien and Thomas A. Shannon, eds., *Catholic Social Thought: Encyclicals and Documents from Pope Leo XIII to Pope Francis,* 3rd ed. (Maryknoll, NY: Orbis Books, 2016). For the most comprehensive compilation of analyses of these documents, see Kenneth R. Himes, OFM, ed., *Modern Catholic Social Teaching:*

Commentaries and Interpretations, 2nd ed. (Washington, DC: George-town University Press, 2018). For a brief explanation, see Kenneth R. Himes, *Responses to 101 Questions on Catholic Social Teaching,* 2nd ed. (Mahwah, NJ: Paulist Press, 2013).

4. See Michael J. Schuck, *That They Be One: The Social Teaching of the Papal Encyclicals, 1740–1989* (Washington, DC: George-town University Press, 1991). See also Schuck's shorter article on the topic, "Early Modern Roman Catholic Social Thought, 1740–1890," in Himes, *Modern Catholic Social Teaching,* 103–29.

5. See "USCCB President's Statement on the Inauguration of Joseph R. Biden, Jr., as the 46th President of the United States of America" (January 20, 2021), https://www.usccb.org/news/2021/usccb -presidents-statement-inauguration-joseph-r-biden-jr-46th-president -united-states.

6. "USCCB President's Statement on the Inauguration of Joseph R. Biden."

7. For a sampling of background information on the drafting of the text, and its ultimate promulgation, see Goodwin, *Team of Rivals,* 459–72; David Herbert Donald, *Lincoln* (New York: Simon and Schuster, 1995), 354–76; H. W. Brands, *The Zealot and the Emancipator: John Brown, Abraham Lincoln and the Struggle for American Freedom* (New York: Doubleday, 2020), 337–59; Allen C. Guelzo, *Abraham Lincoln: Redeemer President* (Grand Rapids: Eerdmans, 1999), 338–51; Matthew Pinsker, *Abraham Lincoln* (Washington, DC: CQ Press, 2002), 130–34, 152–57, 209–12.

8. Ibram X. Kendi, *How to Be an Antiracist* (New York: One World, 2019), 13.

9. Abraham Lincoln, "To Horace Greeley," in *The Collected Works of Abraham Lincoln,* vol. 5, ed. Roy. P. Basler (New Brunswick, NJ: Rutgers University Press, 1953), 388. It is at least worth noting, however, that the views Lincoln expressed in this letter ought to be separated from what he believed as an individual vis-à-vis slavery. He continued, "I have here stated my purpose according to my view of *official* duty. I intend no modification of my oft-expressed *personal* wish that all men everywhere could be free." No doubt, this admission of the separation of personal and professional opinion would not have appeased abolitionists.

10. Cited in Charles Silberman, *Crisis in Black and White* (New York: Random House, 1964), 92–93.

11. Frederick Douglass, "Lincoln and the Colored Troops," in *Reminiscences of Abraham Lincoln*, ed. Allen Thorndike Rice (New York: Harper and Brothers, 1909), 323.

12. Goodwin, *Team of Rivals*, 207–8. Goodwin concludes, "There is no way to penetrate Lincoln's personal feelings about race. There is, however, the fact that armies of scholars, meticulously investigating every aspect of his life, have failed to find a single act of racial bigotry on his part" (207).

13. Widely regarded as the "father of Latin American liberation theology," Gustavo Gutiérrez wrote the seminal text of the movement a century after Lincoln's death. See his *A Theology of Liberation: History, Politics, and Salvation*, trans. Sister Caridad Inda and John Eagleson (Maryknoll, NY: Orbis Books, 1973).

14. Phillip Berryman, *Liberation Theology: The Essential Facts about the Revolutionary Movement in Latin America and Beyond* (New York: Pantheon Books, 1987), 6.

15. Leonard Boff and Clodovis Boff, *Introducing Liberation Theology*, trans. Paul Burns (Maryknoll, NY: Orbis Books, 1987), 61–63.

16. M. Shawn Copeland, *Knowing Christ Crucified: The Witness of African American Religious Experience* (Maryknoll, NY: Orbis Books, 2018), 9.

17. Copeland, *Knowing Christ Crucified*, 83. As Guelzo notes in *Abraham Lincoln*, "The Emancipation Proclamation has been set down as a half-hearted effort, partly because it was, after all, not a declaration of national abolition, and partly because the authority the proclamation was predicated upon was only the military necessity of the war" (343–44).

18. See Philip L. Ostergard, *The Inspired Wisdom of Abraham Lincoln: How Faith Shaped an American President—and Changed the Course of a Nation* (Carol Stream, IL: Tyndale House, 2008), 186–92.

19. See Cyprian Davis, *The History of Black Catholics in the United States* (New York: Crossroad, 1990), 117–22. As Davis points out, the Roman curia held a much more positive view toward Black Catholics, and Black people in general, which resulted in a much more progressive view in favor of emancipation.

20. Cited in Brands, *The Zealot and the Emancipator*, 333.

21. For more on the primaries and general election of 1860, see Goodwin, *Team of Rivals*, 237–78; and Donald, *Lincoln*, 230–56.

22. Boff and Boff, *Introducing Liberation Theology*, 62.

23. I do not mean to insinuate that Lincoln covered as much ground theologically as the foundational figures in liberation theology.

24. In fact, Lincoln deserves far more attention than only this brief section of the present chapter. Nevertheless, this foundation will be important for understanding Lincoln through the lens of a tradition to which he did not belong, but toward which he was not nearly as hostile as other presidents before and after his time.

25. See John T. Noonan Jr., *A Church That Can and Cannot Change: The Development of Catholic Moral Teaching* (Notre Dame, IN: University of Notre Dame Press, 2005). On the particular development of Church teaching on slavery, see 17–123 and 228–62.

26. See Noonan, *A Church That Can and Cannot Change*, 36–41.

27. Davis, *History of Black Catholics in the United States*, 40.

28. For only a sampling of examples, see Christopher Lamb, *The Outsider: Pope Francis and His Battle to Reform the Church* (Maryknoll, NY: Orbis Books, 2020), 147–67; Austen Ivereigh, *Wounded Shepherd: Pope Francis and His Struggle to Convert the Catholic Church* (New York: Henry Holt and Company, 2019), 303–5.

29. Davis, *History of Black Catholics in the United States*, 40. Davis goes into great detail on this issue on 28–66. See also Copeland, *Knowing Christ Crucified*, 87–95.

30. See Noonan, *A Church That Can and Cannot Change*, 108. This has also been a tactic of some American bishops during Francis's pontificate. One very obvious lie was that some U.S. bishops (who remained anonymous) claimed that Francis had critiqued the pastoral ministry of Fr. James Martin to the LGBTQ+ community. On this claim, see J. D. Flynn, "US Bishops: Pope Francis Talks Fr. James Martin, Euthanasia, at Private Meeting," *Catholic News Agency*, February 20, 2020, https://www.catholicnewsagency.com/news/43635/us-bishops -pope-francis-talks-fr-james-martin-euthanasia-at-private-meeting. For the correction of this report, see Archbishop John Wester, "Archbishop Wester Responds to Recounting of Pope's Words about Jesuit Fr. James Martin," *National Catholic Reporter*, February 21, 2020, https://www .ncronline.org/news/people/archbishop-wester-responds-recounting -popes-words-about-jesuit-fr-james-martin. For Pope Francis's own letter of support to Fr. Martin, see Christopher Lamb, "Pope Praises James Martin's Ministry to Gay Catholics," *The Tablet*, June 27, 2021,

https://www.thetablet.co.uk/news/14258/pope-praises-james-martin-s
-ministry-to-gay-catholics.

31. Vatican II, Pastoral Constitution on the Church in the Modern World, *Gaudium et Spes* (December 7, 1965). Pope John Paul II made clear in his 1993 encyclical *Veritatis Splendor* that slavery and all of the other offenses listed by the Council fathers were intrinsically evil or could never be justified (see no. 80).

32. Noonan, *A Church That Can and Cannot Change*, 117.

33. See James Hennesey, *American Catholics: A History of the Roman Catholic Community in the United States* (Oxford: Oxford University Press, 1981), 148–49.

34. For an excellent overview of Christian conversion, see Michael E. Lee, *Revolutionary Saint: The Theological Legacy of Óscar Romero* (Maryknoll, NY: Orbis Books, 2018), 44–85.

35. See Noonan, *A Church That Can and Cannot Change*, 119–23.

36. W. Dale Mason, "The Indian Policy of Abraham Lincoln," in *Indigenous Policy Journal* 20, no. 3 (Fall 2009): 2. See also Sherry Salway Black, "Lincoln: No Hero to Native Americans," in *Washington Monthly*, January/February 2013, https://washingtonmonthly.com/2012/12/27/lincoln-no-hero-to-native-americans/.

37. Mason, "The Indian Policy of Abraham Lincoln," 4.

38. Lee, *Revolutionary Saint*, 126.

39. See Gutiérrez, *A Theology of Liberation*, 29–33.

40. See Pope Francis, *Fratelli Tutti* (October 3, 2020), https://www.vatican.va/content/francesco/en/encyclicals/documents/papa-francesco_20201003_enciclica-fratelli-tutti.html.

41. The crisis to which Francis refers is the throwaway culture in which we live today. This manifests itself not only in wasting money and resources, but human beings. As he writes in the previous paragraph of *Laudato Si'*, "The current model, with its emphasis on success and self-reliance, does not appear to favor an investment in efforts to help the slow, the weak or the less talented to find opportunities in life" (no. 196), citing his own apostolic exhortation, *Evangelii Gaudium* (November 24, 2013), no. 209.

42. All citations will come from *The Spiritual Exercises of St. Ignatius: Based on Studies in the Language of the Autograph*, ed. Louis J. Puhl (Chicago: Loyola Press, 1951) and will be cited parenthetically by section number. For a helpful, popular explanation of

these principles, see James Martin, *The Jesuit Guide to (Almost) Everything: A Spirituality for Real Life* (New York: HarperCollins, 2010), 231–65.

43. For the most precise argument against such a claim, see David Carroll Cochran, *Catholic Realism and the Abolition of War* (Maryknoll, NY: Orbis Books, 2014). For his treatment of slavery, see 133–48.

44. Here, one is reminded of the famous quote from Dom Helder Camara: "When I give food to the poor, they call me a saint. When I ask why they are poor, they call me a Communist."

45. See Goodwin, *Team of Rivals*, 728.

46. There is clearly a parallel here to describing Lincoln as magnanimous. For more on this point, see Joseph R. Fornieri, *Abraham Lincoln: Philosopher Statesman* (Carbondale: Southern Illinois University Press, 2014), 108–28.

47. Cited in Goodwin, *Team of Rivals*, 700.

48 Cited in Goodwin, *Team of Rivals*, 700.

49. Cited in Goodwin, *Team of Rivals*, 698.

50. For more on the origins of the term, see George E. Demacopoulos, *The Invention of Peter: Apostolic Discourse and Papal Authority in Late Antiquity* (Philadelphia: University of Pennsylvania Press, 2013), 90.

51. It is only fair to note that this feeling was certainly not universal among all of the bishops of the country. Many bishops expressed a more measured tone concerning Biden's candidacy, at least two of them (Cardinal Joseph Tobin, CSsR, of Newark, NJ, and Bishop John Stowe, OFM Conv, of Lexington, KY) clearly indicating that Biden was their preference over the incumbent, Donald Trump.

52. United States Conference of Catholic Bishops, *Forming Consciences for Faithful Citizenship: A Call to Political Responsibility from the Catholic Bishops of the United States* (Washington, DC: USCCB, 2019), https://www.usccb.org/issues-and-action/faithful-citizenship/upload/forming-consciences-for-faithful-citizenship.pdf.

53. Reinhold Niebuhr, *The Irony of American History* (New York: Charles Scribner's Sons, 1952), 145.

54. See Emily Reimer-Barry, "Another Pro-Life Movement Is Possible," *CTSA Proceedings* 75 (2019): 21–41; and Charles C. Camosy, *Beyond the Abortion Wars: A Way Forward for a New Generation* (Grand Rapids: Eerdmans, 2015), 4–6.

55. Camosy, *Beyond the Abortion Wars,* 27. He shows the results of a number of polls that make clear that the vast majority of Americans want greater limits placed on abortion, but even the vast majority of "pro-life" Americans believe that there ought to be some cases, such as when the health of the mother is in jeopardy, or when she has been raped or is the victim of incest, when abortion should be legal.

56. See Richard A. McCormick, *Corrective Vision: Explorations in Moral Theology* (Kansas City, MO: Sheed & Ward, 1994), 189.

57. Julie Hanlon Rubio, *Hope for Common Ground: Mediating the Personal and Political in a Divided Church* (Washington, DC: Georgetown University Press, 2016), 179. On the same page, Rubio writes, that there must be a "shift in focus from cooperation with evil (e.g., trying to change permissive laws allowing abortion) to cooperation with good (working toward reducing abortion by preventing unwanted pregnancies and enhancing option when unwanted pregnancies occur)."

58. See Rubio, *Hope for Common Ground,* 161.

59. McCormick presents twenty such elements. While space does not allow me to address all of them here, for the full list, see McCormick, *Corrective Vision,* 191–200. Indeed, McCormick acknowledges that not "all or many now factually agree on these points. I mean that there is solid hope that they can be brought to agreement" (191). Even this hope may be unfounded in some cases.

60. McCormick, *Corrective Vision,* 194.

61. McCormick, *Corrective Vision,* 194.

62. McCormick, *Corrective Vision,* 200.

63. Sebastian Gomes, "Bishop McElroy: Abortion Is a Preeminent Issue for Catholics. But Not the Only One," *America,* October 19, 2020, https://www.americamagazine.org/politics-society/2020/10/16/bishop-mcelroy-catholic-voters-common-abortion-election.

64. In recent years, this controversy first arose with the presidential candidacy of John Kerry in 2004. For a helpful historical overview of the issue of bishops sanctioning politicians, see John W. O'Malley, *Catholic History for Today's Church: How Our Past Illuminates Our Present* (Lanham, MD: Rowman and Littlefield, 2015), 183–89.

65. Pope Francis, "Meeting with the Bishops of the United States of America" (September 23, 2015), https://www.vatican.va/content/francesco/en/speeches/2015/september/documents/papa-francesco_20150923_usa-vescovi.html.

Chapter Two: Martin Luther King Jr. and Black Lives Matter

1. Coretta Scott King, *My Life with Martin Luther King, Jr.*, rev. ed. (New York: Henry Holt and Company, 1993), 301–2. These words were initially delivered shortly after King's assassination, at Ebenezer Baptist Church, during a press conference.

2. See "Mission/Action Statement," Kings Bay Plowshares 7, https://kingsbayplowshares7.org/mission/.

3. See Barbara Reynolds, "I Was a Civil Rights Activist in the 1960s. But It's Hard for Me to Get Behind Black Lives Matter," *Washington Post*, August 24, 2015, https://www.washingtonpost.com/posteverything/wp/2015/08/24/i-was-a-civil-rights-activist-in-the-1960s-but-its-hard-for-me-to-get-behind-black-lives-matter/.

4. See Olga M. Segura, *Birth of a Movement: Black Lives Matter and the Catholic Church* (Maryknoll, NY: Orbis Books, 2021).

5. Bryan Massingale, *Racial Justice and the Catholic Church* (Maryknoll, NY: Orbis Books, 2010), 140–43.

6. See Malcolm X, "The Ballot or the Bullet," lecture delivered at King Solomon Baptist Church, Detroit, April 12, 1964, https://americanradioworks.publicradio.org/features/blackspeech/mx.html.

7. In what follows in these pages, I will be relying heavily on the following texts that place King in the context of the civil rights movement: David J. Garrow, *Bearing the Cross: Martin Luther King, Jr., and the Southern Christian Leadership Conference* (New York: William Morrow and Company, 1986); Thomas F. Jackson, *From Civil Rights to Human Rights: Martin Luther King, Jr., and the Struggle for Economic Justice* (Philadelphia: University of Pennsylvania Press, 2007); Andrew Young, *An Easy Burden: The Civil Rights Movement and the Transformation of America* (New York: Harper Collins, 1996); and three volumes from Taylor Branch: *Parting the Waters: America in the King Years, 1954–63* (New York: Simon and Schuster, 1988); *Pillar of Fire: America in the King Years, 1963–65* (New York: Simon and Schuster, 1998); and *At Canaan's Edge: America in the King Years, 1965–68* (New York: Simon and Schuster, 2006). It is also worth noting that there was widespread resentment of him in the wider movement as well—Ella Baker thought he was a glory hog and disagreed with his "great individual" style of leadership, SNCC thought he was

too vanilla after a while, the Nation of Islam mocked him all the time, and even the Freedom Riders ridiculed him. Some argued that his stature was both a commentary on his rhetorical skills and expertise in nonviolence but also revealed a patriarchal streak in culture that exalts a great man among a movement of millions. See David Dennis Jr., "A Freedom Rider Recalls Martin Luther King, Jr. and the Complex Ride to Civil Rights," *The Undefeated*, January 16, 2017, https://theundefeated.com/features/a-freedom-rider-recalls-martin-luther-king-jr-and-the-complex-ride-to-civil-rights/; and Gwendolyn Zoharah Simmons, "Martin Luther King, Jr. Revisited: A Black Power Feminist Pays Homage to the King," *Journal of Feminist Studies in Religion* 24, no. 2 (Fall 2008): 189–213.

8. Young, *An Easy Burden*, 353. See also, Branch, *Pillar of Fire*, 593.

9. Martin Luther King Jr., "Where Do We Go from Here?" in *A Testament of Hope: The Essential Writings and Speeches of Martin Luther King, Jr.*, ed. James Melvin Washington (New York: Harper Collins, 1986), 250.

10. King, "Where Do We Go from Here?," 251.

11. See David Levering Lewis, *King: A Biography* (Baltimore: Penguin Books, 1970), 210–11.

12. Lewis, *King*, 215.

13. Jackson, *From Civil Rights to Human Rights*, 171. For more on the aforementioned civil rights bill introduced by Kennedy, see 166–71.

14. James H. Cone, "Preface to the 1989 Edition," in *Black Theology and Black Power*, 50th anniv. ed. (Maryknoll, NY: Orbis Books, 2018), xxvi.

15. Branch, *At Canaan's Edge*, 771.

16. See Ernest Shaw Lyght, *The Religious and Philosophical Foundations in the Thought of Martin Luther King, Jr.* (New York: Vantage Press, 1972), 33–46; and Rufus Burrow Jr., *God and Human Dignity: The Personalism, Theology, and Ethics of Martin Luther King, Jr.* (Notre Dame, IN: University of Notre Dame Press, 2006).

17. Cone, *Black Theology and Black Power*, 64.

18. Martin Luther King Jr., *Stride toward Freedom: The Montgomery Story* (New York: Harper and Brothers, 1958), 102–3. In reviewing these six characteristics, it is instructive how ideologically similar

King is with Day and Merton, along with many others who practiced their commitment to nonviolence in their daily actions for justice.

19. King, *Stride toward Freedom*, 103–4.

20. Cited in Cone, *Black Theology and Black Power*, 55.

21. James H. Cone, *A Black Theology of Liberation*, 20th anniv. ed. (Maryknoll, NY: Orbis Books, 1990), 37.

22. See two reflections on the types of love in King, *Stride toward Freedom*, 104, and in his "Christmas Sermon on Peace" delivered on Christmas Eve, 1967, at Ebenezer Baptist Church in Atlanta. See Martin Luther King Jr., *The Trumpet of Conscience* (New York: Harper and Row, 1968), 72–73.

23. King, *Stride toward Freedom*, 104.

24. King, *The Trumpet of Conscience*, 73.

25. Edward Collins Vacek, *Love, Human and Divine: The Heart of Christian Ethics* (Washington, DC: Georgetown University Press, 1994), 162.

26. King, *The Trumpet of Conscience*, 73–74.

27. King, *Stride toward Freedom*, 105.

28. Francis cites the Golden Rule (Matt 7:12) explicitly in chapter 2 of *Fratelli Tutti*, which he devotes entirely to the story of the Good Samaritan (see no. 60). Unlike Pope Francis, I have chosen to refer to the passage as the "story" rather than the "parable" of the Good Samaritan. For a distinction between these terms, see Marcus Mescher, *The Ethics of Encounter: Christian Neighbor Love as a Practice of Solidarity* (Maryknoll, NY: Orbis Books, 2020), 36n3. A simple search on the Vatican website indicates that Francis has used the term *throwaway culture* on dozens of occasions. It is one of the most enduring themes of his pontificate. He uses it with great variety also, to refer to the elderly, the poor, wasted food, and the natural environment, among others.

29. King, *Stride toward Freedom*, 105.

30. King, *The Trumpet of Conscience*, 74. For the numerous overlaps with Gandhian nonviolence, see Mahatma Gandhi, *All Men Are Brothers: Autobiographical Reflections*, ed. Krishna Kripalani (New York: Continuum, 1980), 81–102. For Gandhi's influence on King, see also Lyght, *The Religious and Philosophical Foundations*, 63–77; and John J. Ansbro, *Martin Luther King, Jr.: The Making of a Mind* (Maryknoll, NY: Orbis Books, 1982), 3–7, 128–46. Ansbro's study is an excellent volume in tracing King's own intellectual history.

31. Martin Luther King Jr., *The Autobiography of Martin Luther King, Jr.*, ed. Clayborne Carson (New York: Warner Books, 1998), 24.

32. King, *Stride toward Freedom*, 105. For obvious allusions to Jesus's instruction in this passage, see Matt 5:41; 18:22.

33. King, *Stride toward Freedom*, 106.

34. See Kevin Ahern, *Structures of Grace: Catholic Organizations Serving the Global Common Good* (Maryknoll, NY: Orbis Books, 2015), 66–70.

35. Here, one could think of the brutal events of Charlottesville, VA, in August 2017, when neo-Nazis and other white supremacists gathered to riot. Many Christian denominations were represented by clergy from their community; conspicuously absent were any Catholic clergy from the area (it is only fair to note that the bishop of the diocese was ill and hospitalized at the time of the incidents, so his own tepid response was delayed). In lieu of the clergy, Eric Martin, a Catholic layperson and theologian (and full disclosure, a friend and colleague), stood on the frontlines, wearing a stole over his shoulders. See Michael Sean Winters, "Hate, Racism Were on One Side in Charlottesville, Not Many," *National Catholic Reporter*, August 14, 2017, https://www.ncronline.org/news/opinion/hate-racism-were-one-side-charlottesville-not-many.

36. See Ellen Frantz, "University Takes Concrete Steps to Support the Black Lives Matter Movement," *The Wood Word*, October 1, 2020, https://www.thewoodword.org/news/2020/10/01/university-takes-concrete-steps-to-support-to-the-black-lives-matter-movement/.

37. Pope Francis in conversation with Austen Ivereigh, *Let Us Dream: The Path to a Better Future* (New York: Simon and Schuster, 2020), 27.

38. In what remains in this chapter, I follow the argument laid out by Olga M. Segura in her volume, *Birth of a Movement: Black Lives Matter and the Catholic Church* (Maryknoll, NY: Orbis Books, 2021).

39. Segura, *Birth of a Movement*, 78.

40. USCCB, "Open Wide Our Hearts," 2018, https://www.usccb.org/resources/open-wide-our-hearts_0.pdf.

41. For the best analysis of the previous documents, see Massingale, *Racial Justice and the Catholic Church*, 43–82.

42. See Cyprian Davis, *The History of Black Catholics in the United States* (New York: Crossroad, 1990). Happily, Davis also makes

mention of the exceptions to the rule and highlights certain bishops who were effective in speaking against racism in the United States.

43. USCCB, "Open Wide Our Hearts," 28–30.

44. Massingale, *Racial Justice and the Catholic Church*, 1. Massingale defines this phenomenon: "Person A, usually but not always white, does something negative to Person B (usually but not always black or Latino) because of the color of his or her skin. This reality is real, but inadequate to deal with the racial quagmires we continue to experience in the United States."

45. Segura, *Birth of a Movement*, 85–86. See also 44–49.

46. The strongest condemnation in "Open Wide Our Hearts" is reserved for "harsh rhetoric that belittles and dehumanizes law enforcement personnel who labor to keep our communities safe. We also condemn violent attacks against police" (5).

47. USCCB, "Open Wide Our Hearts," 29.

48. Garrow, *Bearing the Cross*, 351–52. Pope Paul VI did address the topic in his social encyclical *Populorum Progressio* (March 26, 1967), nos. 62–63.

49. See Charles R. Gallagher, "The Catholic Church, Martin Luther King Jr., and the March in St. Augustine," *Florida Historical Quarterly* 83, no. 2 (Fall 2004): 149–72, at 164n35. This entire article chronicles, in part, the disgraceful treatment King received at the hands of Archbishop Joseph P. Hurley.

50. I discuss Maritain at some length later, with regard to his influence on Dorothy Day.

51. Martin Luther King Jr. "Jacques Maritain" (February 20–May 4, 1951), in *The Papers of Martin Luther King, Jr.* vol. 1, *Called to Serve: January 1929–June 1951*, ed. Ralph E. Luker and Penny A. Russell (Berkeley: University of California Press, 1992), 439.

52. Segura, *Birth of a Movement*, 128. One note: I believe that Segura's use of the term "USCCB's antiracism group" is a misnomer, since the group does not fit the definition of *antiracism* that Kendi employs in *How to Be an Antiracist*, which I discussed in chapter 1. Nevertheless, Segura's use of the term in her third step is absolutely in line with Kendi's definition.

53. See Martin Luther King Jr., *Where Do We Go from Here? Chaos or Community?* (New York: Harper and Row, 1967), 193–202.

54. King, *Where Do We Go from Here?*, 193.

55. See Massingale, *Racial Justice and the Catholic Church*, 120–25.

56. King, *Where Do We Go from Here?*, 197.

57. See Jackson, *From Civil Rights to Human Rights*, 270–75.

58. See King, *Where Do We Go from Here?*, 198. King writes, "Universities adapting to the new needs of the day must learn how to develop the abilities of people who have had trouble with school in their youth and have not earned their credentials" (198).

59. For more on this phenomenon, see Stephen Katsourous, *Come to Believe: How the Jesuits Are Reinventing Education (Again)* (Maryknoll, NY: Orbis Books, 2017).

60. See G. R. Kearney, *More Than a Dream: The Christo Rey Story; How One School's Vision Is Changing the World* (Chicago: Loyola Press, 2008).

61. King, *Where Do We Go from Here?*, 200.

62. See John Gehring, "Vow of Silence? U.S. Bishops Are Quiet on Voting Restrictions," *Commonweal*, April 23, 2021, https://www .commonwealmagazine.org/vow-silence.

63. King, *Where Do We Go from Here?*, 202.

64. Massingale, *Racial Justice and the Catholic Church*, 40–41.

65. On the importance of passion in Church teaching, see Massingale, *Racial Justice and the Catholic Church*, 77.

Chapter Three: Dorothy Day and Environmental Personalism

1. Daniel Berrigan, *Portraits of Those I Love* (New York: Crossroad, 1982), 88. In this passage, Berrigan was writing in the wake of the first Plowshares action, in which he and seven others broke into the General Electric plant in King of Prussia, PA, in September 1980, beating two nuclear warheads in an attempt to fulfill the prophecy of Isaiah to "beat swords into plowshares." It is to this group that Berrigan refers in the epigraph cited here.

2. David J. O'Brien, "The Pilgrimage of Dorothy Day," *Commonweal* 107 (December 19, 1980): 711–15, at 711.

3. See Mark S. Massa, *Catholics and American Culture: Fulton Sheen, Dorothy Day, and the Notre Dame Football Team* (New York: Crossroad, 1999), 102–27.

4. To be certain, Merton and King also paid great prices for their commitment to nonviolence, but in King's case, he was targeted especially because of his role in the civil rights movement. Questions about Merton's "searching" in Eastern religions had been critical in his being considered persona non grata among the U.S. Catholic bishops. For more on this point, see "Merton: Persona non Grata," in *Commonweal*, March 7, 2005, https://www.commonwealmagazine.org/merton -persona-non-grata.

5. See Jim Forest, *All Is Grace: A Biography of Dorothy Day* (Maryknoll, NY: Orbis Books, 2011), 156.

6. Forest, *All Is Grace*, 162.

7. Marc H. Ellis, "Peter Maurin: To Bring the Social Order to Christ," in *Revolution of the Heart: Essays on the Catholic Worker*, ed. Patrick G. Coy (Philadelphia: Temple University Press, 1988), 23.

8. For the best summary and analysis of the encyclical, see Thomas A. Shannon, "Commentary on *Rerum Novarum* (*The Condition of Labor*)," in *Modern Catholic Social Teaching: Commentaries and Interpretations*, ed. Kenneth R. Himes, OFM, 2nd ed. (Washington, DC: Georgetown University Press, 2018), 133–57.

9. For a helpful overview of the first five years of Francis's pontificate on labor, see Thomas Massaro, *Mercy in Action: The Social Teachings of Pope Francis* (Lanham, MD: Rowman and Littlefield, 2018), 45–67.

10. Dorothy Day, *The Long Loneliness* (San Francisco: Harper Collins, 1952), 204.

11. Pope Francis, "Audience to Representatives of the Communications Media" (March 16, 2013), http://www.vatican.va/content/ francesco/en/speeches/2013/march/documents/papa-francesco _20130316_rappresentanti-media.html.

12. Day, *The Long Loneliness*, 205.

13. Ruma Paul, "Local Mayor Suspended as Bangladesh Disaster Toll Climbs to 430," *Reuters*, May 2, 2013, https://www.reuters.com/ article/us-bangladesh-building/local-mayor-suspended-as-bangladesh -disaster-toll-climbs-to-430-idUSBRE9410CU20130502.

14. Pope Francis, "No to 'Slave Labour'" (May 1, 2013), http://www.vatican.va/content/francesco/en/cotidie/2013/documents/papa-francesco-cotidie_20130501_slave-labour.html.

15. Dorothy Day, "Blood on Our Coal," *The Catholic Worker*, December 1946. Cited in Robert Ellsberg, ed., *Dorothy Day: Selected Writings* (Maryknoll, NY: Orbis Books, 2005), 250.

16. Dorothy Day, "Reflections on Work," *The Catholic Worker*, March 1947, https://www.catholicworker.org/dorothyday/articles/452.html.

17. Day, *The Long Loneliness*, 210.

18. Dorothy Day, "Of Justice and Breadlines," *The Catholic Worker*, January 1972, cited in Ellsberg, *Dorothy Day: Selected Writings*, 252–53.

19. Christine Firer Hinze, *Radical Sufficiency: Work, Livelihood, and a US Catholic Economic Ethic* (Washington, DC: Georgetown University Press, 2021), 50.

20. See Bryan Massingale, *Racial Justice and the Catholic Church* (Maryknoll, NY: Orbis Books, 2010), 77.

21. James T. Fisher, *Communion of Immigrants: A History of Catholics in America* (New York: Oxford University Press, 2008), 147.

22. Pope Francis, "Address to the Members of the Movement of Christian Workers" (January 16, 2016), http://www.vatican.va/content/francesco/en/speeches/2016/january/documents/papa-francesco_20160116_movimento-cristiano-lavoratori.html.

23. Fisher, *Communion of Immigrants*, 148.

24. See Charles E. Curran, *The Social Mission of the U.S. Catholic Church: A Theological Perspective* (Washington, DC: Georgetown University Press, 2011), 118–20.

25. Curran, *The Social Mission of the U.S. Catholic Church*, 119.

26. Curran, *The Social Mission of the U.S. Catholic Church*, 120–21.

27. Pope Francis, "Address to the Participants in the World Meeting of Popular Movements" (October 28, 2014), https://www.vatican.va/content/francesco/en/speeches/2014/october/documents/papa-francesco_20141028_incontro-mondiale-movimenti-popolari.html.

28. See Curran, *The Social Mission of the U.S. Catholic Church*, 120.

29. Forest, *All Is Grace*, 252.

30. The chair was identified as a chair-cane by Eileen Egan, who had accompanied Day to this protest. See her "Dorothy Day: Pilgrim of Peace," in *Revolution of the Heart: Essays on the Catholic Worker*, ed. Patrick G. Coy (Philadelphia: Temple University Press, 1988), 106.

31. Cited in Daniel Berrigan, *Ten Commandments for the Long Haul* (Nashville: Abingdon Press, 1981), 22.

32. Cited in Ellsberg, *Dorothy Day: Selected Writings*, 253.

33. For more on this point, see Christopher Lamb, *The Outsider: Pope Francis and His Battle to Reform the Church* (Maryknoll, NY: Orbis Books, 2020).

34. Pope Francis, Homily "Work Is the Vocation of Man" (May 1, 2020), https://www.vatican.va/content/francesco/en/cotidie/2020/documents/papa-francesco-cotidie_20200501_illavoro-primavocazione-delluomo.html.

35. There are some notable exceptions. See, e.g., Peter Feuerherd, *The Radical Gospel of Bishop Thomas Gumbleton* (Maryknoll, NY: Orbis Books, 2019); John Gehring, "Traditional Disobedience: Renewing the Legacy of Catholic Activism," *Commonweal*, May 22, 2018, https://www.commonwealmagazine.org/traditional-disobedience.

36. See Pope Francis in conversation with Austen Ivereigh, *Let Us Dream: The Path to a Better Future* (New York: Simon and Schuster, 2020), 27.

37. See Firer Hinze, *Radical Sufficiency*, 282–99.

38. See Forest, *All Is Grace*, 304–15; Robert Ellsberg, "Called to Be Saints: Why I Support the Canonization of Dorothy Day," *America*, April 22, 2015, https://www.americamagazine.org/faith/2015/04/22/called-be-saints-why-i-support-canonization-dorothy-day.

39. Ellsberg, *Dorothy Day: Selected Writings*, 257.

40. For a larger treatment of these and other issues, see James F. Keenan, *University Ethics: How Colleges Can Build and Benefit from a Culture of Ethics* (Lanham, MD: Rowman and Littlefield, 2015); and Gerald J. Beyer, *Just Universities: Catholic Social Teaching Confronts Corporatized Higher Education* (New York: Fordham University Press, 2021).

41. Pope Francis in conversation with Austen Ivereigh, *Let Us Dream*, 116–17.

42. Pope Francis in conversation with Austen Ivereigh, *Let Us Dream*, 117.

43. Mel Piehl, *Breaking Bread: The Catholic Worker and the Origin of Catholic Radicalism in America* (Philadelphia: Temple University Press, 1982), x.

44. Drew Christiansen, "Commentary on *Pacem in Terris (Peace on Earth),*" in *Modern Catholic Social Teaching: Commentaries and Interpretations,* ed. Kenneth R. Himes, 2nd ed. (Washington, DC: Georgetown University Press, 2018), 227.

45. Forest, *All Is Grace,* 157.

46. Robert Ellsberg, ed., *All the Way to Heaven: The Selected Letters of Dorothy Day* (Milwaukee: Marquette University Press, 2010), 75.

47. Reprinted in Robert Ellsberg, ed., *By Little and By Little: Dorothy Day, Selected Writings* (Maryknoll, NY: Orbis Books, 2005), 262.

48. Pius writes, "If therefore a body representative of the people and a government—both having been chosen by free elections—in a moment of extreme danger decide by legitimate instruments of internal and external policy, on defensive precautions, they do not act immorally; so that no Catholic citizen can invoke his conscience in order to refuse to serve and fulfill those duties the law imposed. On this matter we feel that we are in perfect harmony with our predecessors." It is worth noting that Pius did rule out all wars of aggression, however. See Kenneth R. Himes, "Pacifism and the Just War Tradition in Roman Catholic Social Teaching," in *One Hundred Years of Catholic Social Thought: Celebration and Challenge,* ed. John A. Coleman (Maryknoll, NY: Orbis Books, 1991), 331.

49. Patricia McNeal, *Harder Than War: Catholic Peacemaking in Twentieth-Century America* (New Brunswick, NJ: Rutgers University Press, 1992), 43.

50. Forest, *All Is Grace,* 231.

51. See https://www.vatican.va/news_services/press/sinodo/documents/bollettino_25_xiii-ordinaria-2012/02_inglese/b33_02.html #FINAL_LIST_OF_PROPOSITIONS.

52. Dorothy Day, *Loaves and Fishes: The Story of the Catholic Worker Movement* (San Francisco: Harper and Row, 1963), 70.

53. See Bryan Massingale, "An Ethical Reflection upon 'Environmental Racism' in the Light of Catholic Social Teaching," in *The Challenge of Global Stewardship: Roman Catholic Responses,* ed. Maura A. Ryan and Todd David Whitmore (Notre Dame, IN: University of Notre Dame Press, 1997), 234–50.

54. This phrase appears many times in the encyclical. Francis sometimes writes "everything is connected" or "everything is related" or "everything is interrelated." See nos. 16, 70, 91, 92, 117, 120, 137, 138, 142, and 240.

55. I should note that there has been no little controversy over this paragraph by a number of ethicists who—not without merit—declare that Francis has reverted into a gender essentialism in the following sentences. The point of this chapter is not to focus on this particular issue, but suffice it to say that this controversial issue could easily detract from the fundamental point Pope Francis is trying to make in these lines: the relationship between human beings and the entirety of creation is one. It is one because God has created all of these things to have material bodies. Furthermore, all of this creation is fundamentally good because God has created it and deemed it be such. The social reality is more dependent upon this fact than on one's masculinity or femininity.

56. See Day, *The Long Loneliness*, 113–66; James Terence Fisher, *The Catholic Counterculture in America, 1933–1962* (Chapel Hill: The University of North Carolina Press, 1989), 1–24; Forest, *All Is Grace*, 74–86; and Terrence C. Wright, *Dorothy Day: An Introduction to Her Life and Thought* (San Francisco: Ignatius Press, 2018), 31–44.

57. Jacques Maritain, *Man and the State* (Chicago: University of Chicago Press, 1951), 107.

58. Charles E. Curran, *Catholic Moral Theology in the United States: A History* (Washington, DC: Georgetown University Press, 2008), 276.

59. Richard M. Gula, *Reason Informed by Faith: Foundations of Catholic Morality* (Mahwah, NJ: Paulist Press, 1989), 73. Emphasis added.

60. Bernard V. Brady, *Essential Catholic Social Thought*, 2nd ed. (Maryknoll, NY: Orbis Books, 2017), 99.

61. See Robert Ellsberg, ed., *The Duty of Delight: The Diaries of Dorothy Day* (Milwaukee: Marquette University Press, 2008), 424.

62. For a similar argument, see Frederick Ferre, "Personalism and the Dignity of Nature," *The Personalist Forum* 2, no. 1 (Spring 1986): 1–28.

63. Francis J. Sicius, "Peter Maurin's Green Revolution," *U.S. Catholic Historian* 26, no. 3 (Summer 2008): 1–14, at 9.

64. Day, *The Long Loneliness*, 280.

65. See Piehl, *Breaking Bread*, 145–80.

66. I say this despite the claim of John Leo to the contrary that the movement had "never been well-grounded intellectually." Miller, *Dorothy Day*, 482. The claim was made in the aftermath of Roger LaPorte's self-immolation outside the United Nations in 1965.

67. A simple perusal of the footnotes in this chapter alone suggest that Day is seriously considered by many theologians and historians and ought not be ignored in the Catholic intellectual tradition. These notes represent only a fraction of the academic research that has been conducted on Day and the Catholic Worker.

68. Piehl, *Breaking Bread*, 179.

Chapter Four: Thomas Merton: American Monasticism or Monastic Americanism?

1. Mark S. Massa, *Catholics and American Culture: Fulton Sheen, Dorothy Day, and the Notre Dame Football Team* (New York: Crossroad, 1999), 53. The entire chapter on Merton (38–56) is very helpful for placing Merton within the context of postwar American Catholicism.

2. Paul Elie, *The Life You Save May Be Your Own: An American Pilgrimage* (New York: Farrar, Straus and Giroux, 2003), 422.

3. Here, Francis cites Pope John Paul II, *Ecclesia in America* (January 22, 1999), no. 27.

4. Walter Conn, *Christian Conversion: A Developmental Interpretation of Autonomy and Surrender* (Mahwah, NJ: Paulist Press, 1986), 198.

5. Thomas Merton, *The Seven Storey Mountain: An Autobiography of Faith* (New York: Harcourt, 1948), 3.

6. Thomas Merton, *Faith and Violence: Christian Teaching and Christian Practice* (Notre Dame, IN: University of Notre Dame Press, 1968), 68.

7. Merton, *The Seven Storey Mountain*, 10.

8. Merton, *The Seven Storey Mountain*, 353. For some additions to Merton's own account, see Elie, *The Life You Save*, 121–24.

9. Merton, *The Seven Storey Mountain*, 352.

10. Thomas Merton, *No Man Is an Island* (Orlando: Harvest, 1955), 259.

11. These were interrupted after the June 24, 2020, audience, first for the usual suspension of the public audiences in the month of July, and then to account for a series of nine catecheses on "healing the world" in the light of the coronavirus pandemic that was raging throughout the world during that time. The catecheses on prayer resumed on October 7, 2020.

12. See Pope Francis, General Audience (March 31, 2021), https://www.vatican.va/content/francesco/en/audiences/2021/documents/papa-francesco_20210331_udienza-generale.html.

13. Nevertheless, Merton is clear that the two are not equivalent: "Nor is contemplation the gift of prophecy, nor does it imply the ability to read the secrets of mens' hearts." Cited in Thomas Merton, *New Seeds of Contemplation* (New York: New Directions, 1961), 11. It is worth noting here that it is possible that Merton may be using the term *prophecy* differently than I define it in the introduction of the present volume. Merton here seems to identify prophecy with soothsayers.

14. See Thomas Merton, "The Inner Experience," in *Thomas Merton: Spiritual Master*, ed. Lawrence S. Cunningham (Mahwah, NJ: Paulist Press, 1992), 294–356.

15. Merton, "The Inner Experience," 307.

16. Michael Mott, *The Seven Mountains of Thomas Merton* (Boston: Houghton Mifflin, 1984).

17. One such time was the summer of 1949. See Mott, *Seven Mountains*, 254.

18. Pope Francis, General Audience (May 12, 2021), https://www.vatican.va/content/francesco/en/audiences/2021/documents/papa-francesco_20210512_udienza-generale.html.

19. James Terence Fisher, *The Catholic Counterculture in America, 1933–1962* (Chapel Hill: University of North Carolina Press, 1989), 216. The monastic life into which Merton entered also places great emphasis on the intellectual life. See Jean Leclercq, *The Love of Learning and the Desire for God: A Study of Monastic Culture*, trans. Catharine Misrahi (New York: Fordham University Press, 1982).

20. Massa, *Catholics and American Culture*, 39.

21. Anne E. Carr, *A Search for Wisdom and Spirit: Thomas Merton's Theology of the Self* (Notre Dame, IN: University of Notre Dame Press, 1988), 6.

22. Mott, *Seven Mountains*, 297.

23. See Fisher, *The Catholic Counterculture*, 222.

24. Massa himself admits that Merton's penchant for contemplation was apparently a "rather un-American virtue." See *Catholics and American Culture*, 41.

25. See Patricia McNeal, *Harder than War: Catholic Peacemaking in Twentieth-Century America* (New Brunswick, NJ: Rutgers University Press, 1992), 115.

26. See Eli S. McCarthy, "Just Peace Ethic: A Virtue-Based Approach," in *A Just Peace Ethic Primer: Building Sustainable Peace and Breaking Cycles of Violence*, ed. Eli S. McCarthy (Washington, DC: Georgetown University Press, 2020), 66–69.

27. The three categories are *jus in conflictione* (engaging conflict); *jus ex bello* (breaking cycles of violence); and *jus ad pacem* (building sustainable peace). See McCarthy, "Just Peace Ethic," 67. The Latin terms were coined by Gerald Schlabach.

28. Merton, *Faith and Violence*, 215.

29. Ignacio Ellacuría, "Christian Spirituality," trans. J. Matthew Ashley, in *Ignacio Ellacuría: Essays on History, Liberation, and Salvation*, ed. Michael E. Lee (Maryknoll, NY: Orbis Books, 2013), 281–82. For more on this point, see Dean Brackley, *The Call to Discernment in Troubled Times: New Perspectives on the Transformative Wisdom of Ignatius of Loyola* (New York: Crossroad, 2004), 224–25.

30. Merton, *Faith and Violence*, 217.

31. See Merton, *New Seeds of Contemplation*, 112–22.

32. See Shawn Francis Peters, *The Catonsville Nine: A Story of Faith and Resistance in the Vietnam Era* (Oxford: Oxford University Press, 2012); and Mark S. Massa, *The American Catholic Revolution: How the Sixties Changed the Church Forever* (Oxford: Oxford University Press, 2010), 103–28.

33. See Peters, *The Catonsville Nine*, 128–30; Mott, *Seven Mountains*, 530; Kristen Tobey, *Plowshares: Protest, Performance, and Religious Identity in the Nuclear Age* (University Park: Pennsylvania State University Press, 2016), 28–29.

34. Thomas Merton, *Passion for Peace: Reflections on War and Nonviolence*, ed. William H. Shannon (New York: Crossroad, 2006), 160, 162.

35. Daniel Berrigan, *Portraits of Those I Love* (New York: Crossroad, 1982), 13.

36. Thomas Merton, *Peace in the Post-Christian Era*, ed. Patricia A. Burton (Maryknoll, NY: Orbis Books, 2004), 102–8.

37. See Charles Meconis, *With Clumsy Grace: The American Catholic Left 1961–1975* (New York: Seabury Press, 1979), 36–38. Even in the case of Gandhi, there is plenty of evidence that he took strategy into account when performing his own actions.

38. Merton, *Conjectures of a Guilty Bystander* (Garden City, NY: Image Books, 1968), 86–87.

39. Merton, *Peace in a Post-Christian Era*, 132–23.

40. Merton, *Conjectures of a Guilty Bystander*, 156.

41. McNeal, *Harder than War*, 117. In these pages, see also the clear line of connection McNeal makes from Gandhi to King to Merton.

42. See Elie, *The Life You Save*, 405.

43. Mott, *Seven Mountains*, 390. Despite the vagaries in Merton's writing on race, there seems to be a consensus among Black thinkers today that Merton was a great ally to Black people in his own time. See Albert Raboteau, "Thomas Merton and Racial Reconciliation," in *The Merton Annual* 21 (2008): 13–24; Peter Feuerherd, "Thomas Merton's Writings on Race Resonate, Gain Renewed Attention in 2020," in *National Catholic Reporter*, December 30, 2020, https://www.ncronline.org/news/people/thomas-mertons-writings-race-resonate-gain-renewed-attention-2020. For some constructive criticism, see Sophfronia Scott, "I Want to Talk to Thomas Merton about Race," in *The Christian Century*, March 11, 2021, https://www.christiancentury.org/article/first-person/i-want-talk-thomas-merton-about-race; and Daniel P. Horan, "Racism Is a White Problem: Thomas Merton, Whiteness and Racial Justice," in *The Merton Annual* 33 (2020): 63–82, esp. 78–81.

44. See Merton, *Faith and Violence*, 121–29.

45. Merton, *Faith and Violence*, 129. On Merton and King as prophetic, see M. Shawn Copeland, "The Watchmen and the Witnesses: Thomas Merton, Martin Luther King, Jr. and the Exercise of the Prophetic," in *The Merton Annual* 30 (2017): 156–70.

46. James H. Cone, *Black Theology and Black Power* (New York: Harper and Row, 1969), 162.

47. Merton, *Faith and Violence*, 129.

48. Cone, *Black Theology and Black Power*, 170. *Kenosis* refers to the self-emptying, especially embodied by Christ. St. Paul counsels the

Philippians: "Let the same mind be in you that was in Christ Jesus, who, though he was in the form of God, did not regard equality with God as something to be exploited, but emptied himself, taking the form of a slave, being born in human likeness. And being found in human form, he humbled himself and became obedient to the point of death—even death on a cross" (2:5–8).

49. See Merton, *Faith and Violence*, 142–44. *Kairos* means "an opportune time."

50. Merton, *Faith and Violence*, 144.

51. I return to this in the final chapter.

52. There is some confusion as to whether the title was *The Seven Storey Mountain* as cited by President Bill Clinton at Lewis's funeral, *USA Today*, July 30, 2020, https://www.usatoday.com/story/news/politics/2020/07/30/bill-clinton-speaks-john-lewis-funeral-full-transcript/5544050002/ or *New Seeds of Contemplation* as recalled by Governor Martin O'Malley in his obituary of Elijah Cummings, *The American Independent*, October 31, 2019, https://americanindependent.com/elijah-cummings-martin-o-malley-baltimore-maryland-democrats-congress/. Lewis himself simply identified it as a book authored by Merton but did not identify which one. See Robert McNamara, "John Lewis: The Books in His Knapsack," *Medium*, March 2, 2015, https://medium.com/@history1800s/john-lewis-the-books-in-his-knapsack-ceec7077080.

53. For a complementary view of this point, see Massimo Faggioli, *Joe Biden and Catholicism in the United States* (New London, CT: Bayard, 2021), 91–124.

54. See David P. Gushee, "Left/Right Polarization as Culture Wars Captivity," in *Polarization in the US Catholic Church: Naming the Wounds, Beginning to Heal*, ed. Mary Ellen Konieczny, Charles C. Camosy, and Tricia C. Bruce (Collegeville, MN: Liturgical Press, 2016), 79. For Francis's document on the Tridentine Mass, see *Traditiones Custodes* (July 16, 2021), which severely limited the celebration of the "Tridentine Rite": https://www.vatican.va/content/francesco/en/motu_proprio/documents/20210716-motu-proprio-traditionis-custodes.html.

55. See Merton, *The Seven Storey Mountain*, 172.

56. Merton, *The Seven Storey Mountain*, 260–61.

57. See chapter 1 for more on this point.

58. Practically, what does this mean about the candidates for whom Catholic may cast a vote? There has been no shortage of discussion about whether Catholics may vote for pro-choice candidates, but in light of Francis's address, one also wonders if they can vote for a candidate that exacerbates poverty, lowers taxes for the rich, etc. How does what he says contrast with what the bishops give us as voting guides?

59. Mott, *Seven Mountains*, 542.

60. Vatican II, Declaration on the Relation of the Church to Non-Christian Religions, *Nostra Aetate* (October 28, 1965). For more on this document, see John W. O'Malley, *What Happened at Vatican II* (Cambridge, MA: Belknap Press, 2008), 218–24; and Mary C. Boys, "What *Nostra Aetate* Inaugurated: A Conversion to the 'Providential Mystery of Otherness,'" *Theological Studies* 74, no. 1 (2013): 73–104.

61. *The Asian Journal of Thomas Merton*, ed. Naomi Burton, Brother Patrick Hart, and James Laughlin (New York: New Directions, 1975), 313. Merton would continue to say that this practice is obligatory for some monks.

62. *The Asian Journal of Thomas Merton*, 316.

63. Thomas Merton, *Contemplation in a World of Action* (New York: Doubleday, 1971), 173.

64. Merton, *Faith and Violence*, 199.

65. See John F. Kavanaugh, *Following Christ in a Consumer Culture*, 25th anniv. ed. (Maryknoll, NY: Orbis Books, 2006).

Chapter Five: Prophecy for Our Country and Time

1. Cited in Elizabeth A. Johnson, ed., *The Church Women Want: Catholic Women in Dialogue* (New York: Crossroad, 2002), 139.

2. See David Tracy, *The Analogical Imagination: Christian Theology and the Culture of Pluralism* (New York: Crossroad, 1981).

3. "In-Flight Press Conference of His Holiness Pope Francis from the United States of America to Rome" (September 27, 2015), https://www.vatican.va/content/francesco/en/speeches/2015/september/documents/papa-francesco_20150927_usa-conferenza-stampa.html.

4. For the best biography of Prejean, see Joyce Duriga, *Helen Prejean: Death Row's Nun* (Collegeville, MN: Liturgical Press, 2017).

Prejean's three volumes are *Dead Man Walking: An Eyewitness Account of the Death Penalty in the United States* (New York: Random House, 1993); *The Death of Innocents: An Eyewitness Account of Wrongful Executions* (New York: Random House, 2005); and *River of Fire: My Spiritual Journey* (New York: Random House, 2019).

5. Prejean, *Dead Man Walking*, 245.

6. Prejean, *Dead Man Walking*, 217.

7. Prejean, *The Death of Innocents*, 55.

8. Prejean, *River of Fire*, 241.

9. See Prejean, *River of Fire*, 243.

10. Prejean, *River of Fire*, 242.

11. As some have noted, today slavery continues in the form of the modern prison system.

12. Duriga, *Helen Prejean*, 24.

13. See Prejean, *River of Fire*, 249–75.

14. Duriga, *Helen Prejean*, 77.

15. Prejean, *River of Fire*, 289.

16. Prejean, *River of Fire*, 290.

17. See Nuri Valbona, "Q & A with Sr. Norma Pimentel: Meeting Pope Francis," *Global Sisters Report*, September 28, 2015, https://www.globalsistersreport.org/blog/q/q-sr-norma-pimentel-meeting-pope-francis-31586.

18. Norma Pimentel, MJ, "Acceptance of the 2019 LCWR Outstanding Leadership Award," 1, https://lcwr.org/sites/default/files/calendar/attachments/award_acceptance_remarks_-_norma_pimental_mj.pdf.

19. Pimentel, "Acceptance of the 2019 LCWR Outstanding Leadership Award," 1.

20. Valbona, "Q & A with Sr. Norma Pimentel."

21. See Joshua J. McElwee, "Vatican Ends Controversial Three-Year Oversight of US Sisters' Leaders," *National Catholic Reporter*, April 16, 2015, https://www.ncronline.org/news/vatican/vatican-ends-controversial-three-year-oversight-us-sisters-leaders.

22. See Soli Salgado and Dan Stockman, "Sr. Norma Pimentel, LCWR Award Recipient, Embraces 'Holy Chaos' of Her Ministry to Migrants," *Global Sisters Report*, August 17, 2019, https://www.globalsistersreport.org/news/ministry-trends/sr-norma-pimentel-lcwr-award-recipient-embraces-holy-chaos-her-ministry.

23. Devin Watkins, "Pope Francis Praises US Nun for Work to Welcome Migrants," *Vatican News*, May 28, 2021, https://www.vaticannews.va/en/pope/news/2021-05/pope-francis-video-message-norma-pimentel-migrants.html.

24. Pope Francis in conversation with Austen Ivereigh, *Let Us Dream*, 100.

25. See Soli Salgado, "Sr. Patricia Chappell Has Long Been a Leader. Now She's Being Honored for It," *Global Sisters Report*, August 3, 2020, https://www.globalsistersreport.org/news/justice/religious-life/news/sr-patricia-chappell-has-long-been-leader-now-shes-being-honored-it.

26. Salgado, "Sr. Patricia Chappell Has Long Been a Leader."

27. Andrew Nelson, "Q&A with Sister Patricia Chappell of Pax Christi," *Georgia Bulletin*, September 27, 2012, https://georgiabulletin.org/news/2012/09/qa-with-sister-patricia-chappell-of-pax-christi/.

28. Francis is citing his own Message for the 2016 World Day of Peace, "Overcome Indifference and Win Peace" (December 8, 2015), https://www.vatican.va/content/francesco/en/messages/peace/documents/papa-francesco_20151208_messaggio-xlix-giornata-mondiale-pace-2016.html. The sentiment, however, is one that Francis has returned to nearly fifty times in various speeches and addresses of his pontificate.

29. Lisa Doris Alexander, *Expanding the Black Film Canon: Race and Genre across Six Decades* (Lawrence: University Press of Kansas, 2019), 119.

30. Christina N. Baker, *Contemporary Black Women Filmmakers and the Art of Resistance* (Columbus: Ohio State University Press, 2018), 28.

31. For the best volume on this injustice, see Michelle Alexander, *The New Jim Crow: Mass Incarceration in the Age of Colorblindness* (New York: New Press, 2010).

32. Juleyka Lantigua-Williams, "Ava DuVernay's *13th* Reframes American History," *The Atlantic*, October 6, 2016, https://www.theatlantic.com/entertainment/archive/2016/10/ava-duvernay-13th-netflix/503075/.

33. For helpful summaries of the plot, see Alexander, *Expanding the Black Film Canon*, 127; and Baker, *Contemporary Black Women Filmmakers*, 113–22.

34. Alexander, *Expanding the Black Film Canon*, 140.

35. See Elizabeth A. Johnson, *Quest for the Living God: Mapping Frontiers in the Theology of God* (New York: Continuum, 2007), 91.

36. Olga M. Segura, "#MeToo Founder Tarana Burke: 'Jesus Was the First Activist That I Knew,'" *Sojourners*, September 24, 2018, https://sojo.net/articles/metoo-founder-tarana-burke-jesus-was-first-activist-i-knew.

37. See Segura, "#MeToo Founder Tarana Burke."

38. Anne M. Clifford, *Introducing Feminist Theology* (Maryknoll, NY: Orbis Books, 2001), 208.

39. Here, I want to avoid one particular reading of Truth's love for white people: that this is the only acceptable response. The problem with such an interpretation is that it may have the effect of minimizing the brutality of slavery, or police the emotions of Black people today. That is not the intent of raising this passage.

40. See Barbara Hilkert Andolsen, *"Daughters of Jefferson, Daughters of Bootblacks": Racism and American Feminism* (Macon, GA: Mercer University Press, 1986), 76.

41. Sojourner Truth, "Ain't I a Woman?," cited in Clifford, *Introducing Feminist Theology*, 158.

42. See Peter J. Longo, *Great Plains Politics* (Lincoln: University of Nebraska Press, 2018), 1–19.

43. See Longo, *Great Plains Politics*, 15.

44. Longo, *Great Plains Politics*, 8.

45. I recognize that Johnson could also have been a part of the first section of this chapter since she is a member of the Sisters of Saint Joseph, Brentwood, but I elected to place her in this section because her primary ministry has been as an academic theologian.

46. See Heidi Schlumpf, *Elizabeth Johnson: Questing for God* (Collegeville, MN: Liturgical Press, 2016), 52. The other woman to graduate with Johnson in 1981 was Mary Ann Fatula, OP. Schlumpf's biography is the best source on Johnson's life.

47. See Elizabeth A. Johnson, *Women, Earth, and Creator Spirit* (Mahwah, NJ: Paulist Press, 1993), 61–68.

48. Elizabeth A. Johnson, *Ask the Beasts: Darwin and the God of Love* (London: Bloomsbury, 2014), 259. The first time I am aware of the term *ecological conversion* being introduced in papal magisterium was during Pope John Paul II's General Audience of January 17, 2001, https://www.vatican.va/content/john-paul-ii/en/audiences/2001/documents/hf_jp-ii_aud_20010117.html.

49. See Schlumpf, *Elizabeth Johnson*, 56–63. This action taken by the board of bishops was extraordinary; they were not in the habit of engaging so dramatically and personally in tenure cases. They chose this battle because Johnson was writing on Mary from a feminist perspective.

50. Schlumpf, *Elizabeth Johnson*, 63.

51. Committee on Doctrine, United States Conference of Catholic Bishops, "Statement on *Quest for the Living God: Mapping Frontiers in the Theology of God*, by Sister Elizabeth A. Johnson," March 24, 2011, in *When the Magisterium Intervenes: The Magisterium and Theologians in Today's Church*, ed. Richard R. Gaillardetz (Collegeville, MN: Liturgical Press, 2012), 199. All of the relevant documents of the Johnson case are available in Gaillardetz's volume, including an introduction and reflection from Gaillardetz, 177–294.

52. "To Speak Rightly of the Living God: Observations by Dr. Elizabeth A. Johnson, CSJ, on the Statement of the Committee on Doctrine of the United States Conference of Catholic Bishops about her book *Quest for the Living God: Mapping Frontiers in the Theology of God*," in Gaillardetz, *When the Magisterium Intervenes*, 249.

53. Elizabeth A. Johnson, *She Who Is: The Mystery of God in Feminist Theological Discourse* (New York: Crossroad, 1992), 223.

54. Johnson, *She Who Is*, 46.

55. Kwok Pui-Lan, "Feminist Theology as Intercultural Discourse," in *The Cambridge Companion to Feminist Theology*, ed. Susan Frank Parsons (Cambridge: Cambridge University Press, 2002), 29.

56. See Pope Francis, "Address at Second World Meeting of Popular Movements" (July 9, 2015), https://www.vatican.va/content/francesco/en/speeches/2015/july/documents/papa-francesco_20150709_bolivia-movimenti-popolari.html.

57. See Pope Francis, "Address at Second World Meeting of Popular Movements."

58. Kwok Pui-Lan, "Engendering Christ," in *The Strength of Her Witness: Jesus Christ in the Global Voices of Women*, ed. Elizabeth A. Johnson (Maryknoll, NY: Orbis Books, 2016), 268.

59. Kwok Pui-Lan, "Reflection on Women's Sacred Scriptures," in *Women's Sacred Scriptures*, ed. Kwok Pui-Lan and Elisabeth Schüssler Fiorenza, *Concilium* 1998/3 (London: SCM Press, 1998), 112.

60. Kwok, "Engendering Christ," 265. One need not necessarily cling to any of the examples Kwok offers in this essay to agree with the basic point that I cite in this passage.

Chapter Six: Becoming Great Americans

1. It is worth noting that Gustavo Gutiérrez refers to a "permanent cultural revolution" in his A *Theology of Liberation*, 15th anniv. ed., trans. Sister Caridad Inda and John Eagleson (Maryknoll, NY: Orbis Books, 1988), 21. He writes, "The goal is not only better living conditions, a radical change of structures, a social revolution; it is much more: the continuous creation, never ending, of a new way to be human, a *permanent cultural revolution*." Emphasis in original.

2. Pope Francis, in conversation with Austen Ivereigh, *Let Us Dream: The Path to a Better Future* (New York: Simon and Schuster, 2020), 13.

3. Pope Francis, "Audience to Representatives of the Communications Media" (March 16, 2013), https://www.vatican.va/content/francesco/en/speeches/2013/march/documents/papa-francesco_20130316_rappresentanti-media.html.

4. Jon Sobrino, *The True Church and the Poor*, trans. Matthew J. O'Connell (Maryknoll, NY: Orbis Books, 1984), 93.

5. Gregory Boyle, *Tattoos on the Heart: The Power of Boundless Compassion* (New York: Free Press, 2010), 190.

6. Ignacio Ellacuría, "The Church of the Poor, Historical Sacrament of Liberation," trans. Margaret D. Wilde, in *Ignacio Ellacuría: Essays on History, Liberation, and Salvation*, ed. Michael E. Lee (Maryknoll, NY: Orbis Books, 2013), 248.

7. Ellacuría, "The Church of the Poor," 248. Emphasis in original.

8. Ellacuría, "The Church of the Poor," 248.

9. Ellacuría, "The Church of the Poor," 249.

10. See Pew Research Center, "U.S. Public Becoming Less Religious," November 3, 2015, https://www.pewforum.org/2015/11/03/u-s-public-becoming-less-religious/.

11. Ellacuría, "The Church of the Poor," 249.

12. See Ellacuría, "The Church of the Poor," 249. He writes, "But on the other hand, the fact that the church cannot and should not be reduced to a pure sociopolitical force, working exclusively from an

ideological locus against unjust structures or giving absolute priority to that work, brings on it incomprehension and attack from those who have embraced personal and political partiality as if it were the whole of humanity."

13. Gutiérrez, A *Theology of Liberation*, 171.

14. Gutiérrez, A *Theology of Liberation*, 172.

15. Ellacuría, "The Church of the Poor," 249.

16. Ellacuría, "The Church of the Poor," 250.

17. Ellacuría, "The Church of the Poor," 250.

18. I intentionally avoid using the word *homilizing* here because that would indicate that the preacher in question had followed the liturgical rubrics by preaching on one or more of the approved scriptural texts from that day's entry in the Lectionary.

19. Matt Hadro, "Pavone: With Transfer Pending, Campaign Work a Matter of 'Conscience,'" *Catholic News Agency*, April 21, 2020, https://www.catholicnewsagency.com/news/44266/pavone-with -transfer-pending-campaign-work-a-matter-of-conscience.

20. Ellacuría, "The Church of the Poor," 250.

21. Ellacuría, "The Church of the Poor," 250. Emphasis in original.

22. Cited in Ellacuría, "The Church of the Poor," 252.

23. Sobrino, *The True Church and the Poor*, 94.

24. See Matt 10:39: "Those who find their life will lose it, and those who lose their life for my sake will find it"; Matt 16:25: "For those who want to save their life will lose it, and those who lose their life for my sake will find it"; Mark 8:35: "For those who want to save their life will lose it, and those who lose their life for my sake, and for the sake of the gospel, will save it"; Luke 9:24: "For those who want to save their life will lose it, and those who lose their life for my sake will save it"; John 12:25: "Those who love their life lose it, and those who hate their life in this world will keep it for eternal life." I repeat passages from each of the four Gospels that are almost identical in their wording to make this point abundantly clear: this is a fundamental part of any reading of the Gospels, and any understanding of Jesus's life and ministry.

25. There are other steps that could have been judged by some to have been more fitting choices here. I recognize some of them in earlier chapters of this volume. Even some of these, I include as part of the ten steps listed here.

Notes

26. Michael Peppard, "Can the Church Transcend a Polarized Culture?" in *Polarization in the US Catholic Church: Naming the Wounds, Beginning to Heal*, ed. Mary Ellen Konieczny, Charles C. Camosy, and Tricia C. Bruce (Collegeville, MN: Liturgical Press, 2016), 149. Peppard then goes on to name some other important realities like a lack of overlap among contributors for ideologically opposed Catholic media.

27. Robert J. Schreiter, *The Ministry of Reconciliation: Spirituality and Strategies* (Maryknoll, NY: Orbis Books, 1998), 127.

28. John C. Dwyer, "Person, Dignity of," in *The New Dictionary of Catholic Social Thought*, ed. Judith A. Dwyer (Collegeville, MN: Liturgical Press, 1994), 734.

29. Pope Francis, *Evangelii Gaudium* (November 24, 2013), https://www.vatican.va/content/francesco/en/apost_exhortations/documents/papa-francesco_esortazione-ap_20131124_evangelii-gaudium.html#_ftnref173.

30. As I mention in chapter 4, Merton claimed not to be a pacifist, but much of his writing speaks to his commitment to complete nonviolence.

31. Pope Francis in conversation with Austen Ivereigh, *Let Us Dream*, 6.

32. Pope Francis in conversation with Austen Ivereigh, *Let Us Dream*, 137.

33. Vatican II, *Sacrosanctum Concilium* (December 4, 1963), https://www.vatican.va/archive/hist_councils/ii_vatican_council/documents/vat-ii_const_19631204_sacrosanctum-concilium_en.html.

34. Dean Brackley, "Higher Standards," *America*, February 6, 2006, https://www.americamagazine.org/issue/559/article/higher-standards.

35. I recognize that Merton's monasticism complicates this point. Nevertheless, Merton's understanding of contemplation and action (see chapter 4) reminds us that prayer itself is an action. It is not a rejection of the world.

36. Pope Francis in conversation with Austen Ivereigh, *Let Us Dream*, 137.

INDEX

Index

Nonviolence, 8, 10, 11, 33, 37–39, 41–42, 50, 52, 64, 78, 80–83, 95, 120
Nonviolent direct action, 33, 80–81
Nuclear weapons, 33–34, 65

Pacem in Terris, 63, 65
Pacifism, 42, 52, 63–66
Pax Christi (organization), 95
Personalism, 38, 67–68
Pimentel, Norma, MJ, 93–94
Polarization within Catholic Church, 84, 113, 117
Political love, 24–26, 28, 118
Political realism, 19, 26
Pontifex, 28, 72, 83–87
Poverty, 48, 65, 66, 109, 112, 119
Prejean, Helen, CSJ, 91–93
Prophets/prophecy, 1–13

Racism and the Church, 20, 22, 34, 45–48, 50, 83
Reconciliation, 82, 83, 117
Rerum Novarum, 20, 52, 54, 60
Role of women in the Church, 90–96, 102, 103, 122
Romero, Óscar, 11, 24

Sacrosanctum Concilium, 122
Sand Creek Massacre, 23
Segura, Olga, 45, 47, 48
Slavery and the Church, 21–23
Solidarity, 43, 44, 60, 93, 100, 110, 111, 112, 118
Spellman, Francis, Cardinal, 46
Supremo Apostolatus Fastigio, 21
Synod of Bishops (2012), 65

Tenderness, 27
Throwaway culture, 40, 56, 60, 62
Triple evils, 36, 42, 45, 50
Trump, Donald, 2, 113
Truth, Sojourner, 98–100

United States Conference of Catholic Bishops (USCCB), 16, 28, 31, 47, 49, 59, 85, 101; *Forming Consciences for Faithful Citizenship,* 28; "Open Wide Our Hearts: The Enduring Call to Love," 45

Vatican II, 22, 63, 122
Vos Estis Lux Mundi, 98
Voting rights, 49, 119

White supremacy, 46, 47, 96, 100, 122